DATE DUE

NO ~~8~~ '94			
DE ~~2~~ '95			
AP ~~15~~ '96			
MR 2 6 '97			
MY 2 7 '98			
~~OC 15~~ '98			
~~MY 17~~ '99			
~~OC 15~~ '00			
DE ~~6~~ '00			
AP 2 1 '05			
FE ~~8~~ '07			
~~MY 1 9~~ '07			

INDIA

FACING THE TWENTY-FIRST CENTURY

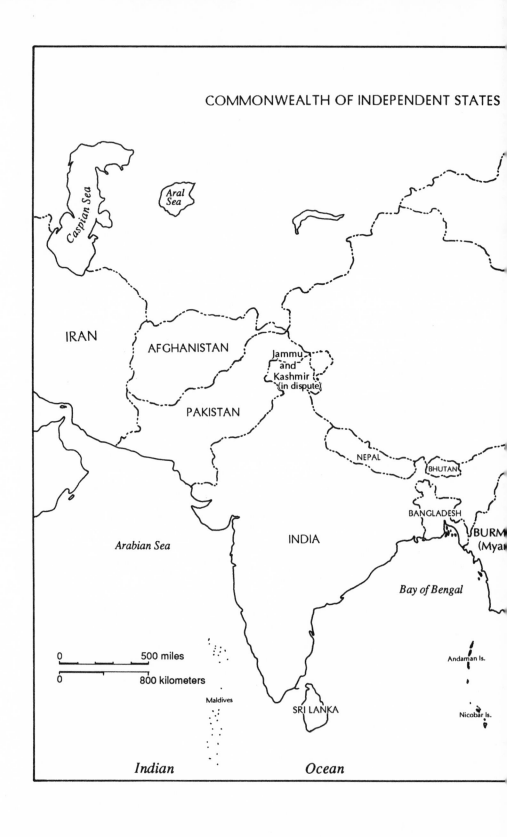

COMMONWEALTH OF INDEPENDENT STATES

Caspian Sea

Aral Sea

IRAN

AFGHANISTAN

Jammu and Kashmir (in dispute)

PAKISTAN

NEPAL

BHUTAN

BANGLADESH

BURM (Mya

Arabian Sea

INDIA

Bay of Bengal

0   500 miles

0   800 kilometers

Andaman Is.

Maldives

SRI LANKA

Nicobar Is.

Indian   Ocean

Lake
Baykal

MONGOLIA

CHINA

(Mar)

LAOS

THAILAND

CAMBODIA

VIETNAM

MALAYSIA

SINGAPORE

NORTH
KOREA

SOUTH
KOREA

Yellow
Sea

Sea
of
Japan

JAPAN

East
China
Sea

TAIWAN

Pacific

Ocean

Philippine
Sea

South China Sea

PHILIPPINES

BRUNEI

MALAYSIA

THE ESSENTIAL ASIA SERIES

David I. Steinberg, editor

INDIA

$\blacklozenge$

FACING THE TWENTY-FIRST
CENTURY

Barbara Crossette

INDIANA UNIVERSITY PRESS
Bloomington • Indianapolis

The paper used in this publication meets the minimum requirements of American National
Standard for Information Sciences—Permanence of Paper for Printed Library Materials, ANSI
Z39.48-1984.

Manufactured in the United States of America

Library of Congress Cataloging-in-Publication Data

Crossette, Barbara.
    India : facing the twenty-first century / Barbara Crossette.
      p. cm. — (The Essential Asia series)
    Includes bibliographical references and index.
    ISBN 0-253-31577-8 (alk. paper).
      1. India—Politics and government—1977- I. Title. II. Series.
DS480.853.C76   1993
954.05'2—dc20   92-35939

1 2 3 4 5 97 96 95 94 93

To the memory of my mother, Elizabeth Lettrich Fretz, and to my father, John Emerson Fretz; they encouraged me to discover worlds beyond my own. To my son, Jonathan, whose generous spirit accepted the nomadic childhood he did not choose. And to my husband, David Wigg, whose forbearance, insights, and constructive criticisms helped shape my reporting in Asia. ✦

CONTENTS

FOREWORD

David I. Steinberg

A DEMOCRACY REQUIRES AN EDUCATED AND INFORMED PUBLIC. This dictum applies as much to foreign policy as to domestic affairs. Yet the American educational system as a whole has sadly neglected foreign affairs and shown little interest in peoples of other countries, although recently it has shown some improvement.

This lack of interest is especially unfortunate in the case of Asia. Asians comprise more than half the world's population, and live in the fastest growing and most economically dynamic area of the globe. In this century, the United States has fought a series of wars in Asia the causes and ramifications of which are still murky to most of the public. Asians have also become a significant minority in U.S. society. There are thus a variety of urgent reasons for better understanding Asia.

There is little excuse for our neglect of the subject. Asia has extremely rich written records, sophisticated oral traditions, extensive archaeological remains, and even a several-centuries'-old tradition of Western scholarship dealing with many parts of the region. There is no reason why the general, informed public should not have access to better information on the diverse societies and cultures of Asia.

Part of the problem is who does the writing. Most works by academicians are so specialized as to be unapproachable, often abstruse, miasmic, inaccessible, and expensive. Those of us in academe and related fields often make excuses for our own and our colleagues' propensity for using arcane and specialist language. Through our writing, we intend not only to convey knowledge precisely, but also to ratify our sense of membership in the particular intellectual clan reflecting our academic disciplines or research interests. Although in the social sciences we my be inured to these pontifications, which we assume will assist in our professional advancement and other desiderata, to inflict them on the public inhibits rather than fosters the spread of knowledge and understanding that we had hoped to impart.

Many years ago I was struck by the fact that an intelligent and engagingly written body of literature existed on a number of European societies, engrossing both the intellect and the emotions and gracefully conveying to the general reader the complexities of those societies. Such volumes combine the accuracy of social science research with the charm of literature, two attributes that need not be in conflict. I was particularly impressed by Barzini's *The Italians*. Writing of such caliber is pitifully lacking for Asia.

Occasionally someone has asked me what single volume one might read for insight into a particular Asian society. I have often been hard pressed to respond, suspecting that their reading time would be relegated to the long airplane passage to Asia, punctuated by meals, movies, and mewling infants. Further, many books, however valid, seemed outdated. Recommending, for example, what I considered to be the best work on Burma—published in 1882—did not seem to be the answer. Neither did suggesting a thoughtful but turgid text, useful in a graduate or undergraduate course for its accurate detail but excruciating in its pace.

Today there is a pressing need to convey to the educated generalist the sense of Asian societies, or at least their most salient characteristics. To do this requires sensitivity both to the society studied and to the proclivities of each author and his or her vision of such a culture. To construct, even if it were possible, a general formula for a series of volumes on disparate societies that would reflect the idiosyncratic diversity of both the societies and the authors seems undesirable.

With the encouragement of the Indiana University Press, we have therefore stimulated a number of authors to write works that maintain individuality and at the same time explain the society in question. Asia *is* essential now more than ever, and we hope this series will highlight that fact and help English-speaking readers to understand the countries covered.

Barbara Crossette's *India* is an example of what some in contemporary America might call "tough love," a sometimes biting but on the whole sympathetic overview by a journalist who knows the country well. Crossette provides important insights into the perplex of cultures and societies that make up the continent called India; her balanced treatment serves as an antidote to much of the "New Age" treacle that has been disseminated about this critically important country and is at the same time more reportorial and more accessible than some other contemporary accounts.

INTRODUCTION

There are those foreigners and strangers who have
loved us, either with tenderness or with a passion.
And there are those who have hated us viciously and
with great malice. But none who have been
indifferent, or just expressed a moderate, routine
interest, a kind of a polite shrug of the shoulders.
There is something in our chemistry which either
attracts the others powerfully, or repels them
comprehensively.

—S. K. Singh, former foreign secretary of India

SOMETIME EARLY IN THE TWENTY-FIRST CENTURY, the turbulent nation of India,
with more than a billion people, will overtake China as the most populous
country on earth. Contrary to the assertion of S. K. Singh—whose division
of the world into those who love India and those who hate it reflects one of
the fantasies that sustain the Indian administrative elite—too many people
are indifferent to the fate of this vast nation rooted in sophisticated civilizations virtually unknown to us. India, furrowed by cultural crosscurrents
unique to the Subcontinent, is the glorious but distant and often too-exotic,
too-romantic land of mythology and epic, of philosophical introspection and
spiritual flight; the home of Rama and Shiva, Gautama Buddha, St. Thomas
the Apostle, Guru Nanak, and dynasties of Muslim sultans and emperors
whose architects transformed the landscape with palaces, gardens, and
tombs. But India is also a modern democracy, the world's largest, and its
political success or failure should concern us; for better or worse, in India's
fate there will be lessons for all democratic nations, including those who
have only recently turned their backs on Communism. If India, increasingly
distancing itself from the Western political culture left behind by colonialism,
can redefine and revitalize democracy in an Indian way, its own way, all the
world wins. If India fails to confront the crises it now faces, or slips deeper
into authoritarianism and militarism to meet the challenges of poverty, caste
ghettoization, regional rebellion, religious strife, and political gangsterism,
there will be those waiting to say that democracy was not compatible with
Indian culture or that India was not ready for it. The world, where one in
every six people is an Indian, would be very much poorer.

As India approaches a new century, the road ahead has never been more obscured by obstacles and doubts. Despite new free-market economic policies, thrust on India in 1991 as much by world events as by a bold government under Prime Minister P. V. Narasimha Rao and his visionary finance minister, Manmohan Singh, this ancient nation remains divided on how to tackle the challenges ahead. A proud people, Indians are generally averse to embracing others' political and economic models, even while they allow traditional institutions to atrophy. Wary of new foreign overlordships of any kind after centuries of subjugation, many Indians lash out at symbols: at the World Bank and International Monetary Fund for their intrusive policy prescriptions and at a host of international human rights groups for turning on the spotlight when desperate security forces go too far in putting down insurrection and dissent.

India, the jewel in the crown of imperial Britain, is now struggling to assert itself as the most important nation between Europe and East Asia economically and strategically, a power that can take its place among the councils of the mighty. It would like to hold a permanent seat in an enlarged United Nations Security Council and be invited to international conclaves to discuss the affairs of distant regions, beginning with the Middle East. It sees for itself a major role in the future of newly independent Central Asia and a voice in Southeast Asia and the Pacific Rim. None of these goals is beyond the reach of New Delhi in the world of new relationships being created on the rubble of the Cold War.

But India must strengthen itself from within before expanding its power abroad, say many of the Indians quoted in the pages of this book. According to indexes measuring the quality of life, and by extension the skills and health of a work force, parts of India are slipping to the levels of Sub-Saharan Africa. In the poorest Indian states, where population is growing at over 2 percent annually—helping to add to the nation each year numbers roughly equal to the total population of Iraq or Australia—literacy is low and malnutrition rising. Nationwide, millions of child laborers are in virtual bondage, denied even a basic education. Yet India must compete for investment with high-literacy, healthier societies like those of Thailand, Malaysia, or, increasingly, Indonesia. On the shop floor, new economic and trade policies may not be enough to lure investors. An educated corps of scientists and engineers, which India has, is not all that industries need.

High on India's social agenda over the next few decades, along with better schooling for children, must be the improvement in the status of women, a factor international development agencies are beginning to stress as a cure for chronic underdevelopment in many countries. Most women in India cannot read; few have control over the size of their families. The majority of Indian girls are denied choices in careers or marriage partners. Women, as well as men, are further restricted by the persistent stranglehold of caste. Girls are also hemmed in by social or religious traditions that inhibit their freedom and personal growth. The attitude toward women cannot be separated from larger discussions now going on in India about how to win-now out of a rich heritage those mindsets and instincts out of step with twenty-first-century thinking while saving the core of an important cultural and spiritual legacy. It has been a grave disappointment to many Indians that in half a century of independence so much optimism about the strength of Indian society has turned to uncertainty and heartbreak.

In 1947, when India won independence from Britain, it was a pioneer and model for the post-colonial age. In the decades that followed, few other countries would match its courage: a poor, illiterate nation riven with ethnic, linguistic, sectarian, and caste divisions daring to choose that most difficult path of all, multiparty parliamentary democracy. No other nation emerging from imperialism had a towering figure like Mohandas Karamchand Gandhi, the Mahatma, whose example of peaceful resistance and nonviolent protest would reach out to inspire the downtrodden worldwide, including those who struggled for civil rights in the American South. Jawaharlal Nehru, India's first prime minister and a leader of the Third World when the geopolitical map was most bipolar, ranked among the great international personalities of his age. Under his tutelage, huge dams were thrown across mighty Subcontinental rivers and steel mills were fired; India would match its moral power with industrial muscle. Among the nations of the world, this one would matter.

Half a century later, India seems bent on self-destruction.

"In the land of Mahatma Gandhi, violence is on the throne today," the eminent jurist Nani Palkhivala wrote recently. "The country with the noblest heritage has become the most criminalized and the most violent democracy in the world." The Congress Party of India's founders, allowed to degenerate into a fractious and undemocratic organization whose grass roots withered from decades of neglect, survives shakily on myths about itself and the nation whose politics it has dominated since independence. Gaps widen daily between the interests of opportunistic politicians of all parties, often allied to the very rich in urban centers, and the needs of that mushrooming population of the deprived, lumbered with their gigantic inequalities and handicaps. At their most pessimistic, Indian social scientists fear that a culture of corruption and easy violence is leading the country into that league of Third World nations with squandered resources and ruined hopes.

Rajni Kothari, who has been studying and analyzing Indian politics and society for more than a quarter of a century, says that in the late 1980s India entered "the worst five years of its history." Corruption exploded frighteningly in scale and sweep, he says in interviews and in his book *State against Democracy*, a harsh critique not only of Indian leadership but also of the negative influences of Western industrial society on India. Corruption, he adds, is a disease that has spread "to all but a very few positions of power." Among its causes is "a pervasive sense of insecurity and uncertainty about the future." Rich or poor, Indians can sense the pressures of dwindling resources and feel the rising social tensions. Frustrated, many are pushing over victory monuments and finding them hollow. Can't India feed itself, a great achievement? Only because of the "abject poverty" in which it allows so many of its people to live, says Mohan Dharia, a local development expert and environmentalist who headed the national planning commission briefly in 1990–91. Others join the iconoclastic chorus: enrollment figures aren't the same as school attendance; words in the Constitution don't necessarily deliver human rights or an independent judiciary; the power of the ballot means little when party goons shoot their way into polling stations; institutions cannot function for the public good when there is no accountability.

What is India? A generation or two removed from the freedom struggle, this complex nation is searching for a way to identify itself or even define itself, as the psychology of secessionism spreads along artificial borders created by imperial Britain. Is this a Hindu nation, the unifying image sought by the newly powerful Bharatiya Janata Party? No and yes. India, where Hindus form more than 60 percent of the population—82 percent if untouchables and tribals who follow no other identifiable belief are counted— is a constitutionally secular country. But cows, sacred to Hindus, cannot be slaughtered in most states and beef does not appear on restaurant menus. Muslim Indians receive official letters and documents bearing "Hindu" dates. Government leaders consult astrologers to choose the most propitious moment to hold an election or be sworn into office. Public buildings are often dedicated with the breaking of coconuts or other temple rites. Hindu India proclaims itself the most open and tolerant society in the world, but is more often, at least officially—and the distinction is important—a mistrustful country deeply suspicious of foreigners and always on the lookout for foreign plots. The Hindu majority can display a baffling minority complex. As "convent schools and Western culture" close in on India, says a pamphlet from the militant Vishwa Hindu Parishad organization, "Hindus have no place to run away."

Indians live on myths, not all of them ancient. Many firmly believed against all evidence that Rajiv Gandhi was the leader who would modernize the country and march it confidently into the twenty-first century. He is dead, victim of a suicidal assassin who reached down to touch his feet in an age-old gesture and detonated a high-tech explosive, the final irony of the Rajiv Gandhi era. Minutes before Rajiv died, he told me in an interview that if returned to power in the election then under way, he would "kill all controversies over religion." But as prime minister from 1984 to 1989, he had done just the opposite. Within hours of his mother's assassination by Sikh bodyguards on October 31, 1984, the new prime minister stood by while mobs fielded by Congress Party colleagues rampaged through New Delhi and other cities, killing thousands of innocent Sikh men and boys. Two years later, Gandhi allowed militant Hindus access to an old mosque, the Babri Masjid, in the holy town of Ayodhya, rekindling a Muslim-Hindu dispute that has subsequently caused the deaths of more than a thousand Indians. When the Supreme Court of India awarded maintenance payments to a divorced Muslim woman, Shah Bano, Gandhi used his huge parliamentary majority to pass a new law denying all Muslim women this right, overriding the progressive judicial ruling, to the delight of Islamic reactionaries and the distress of many other Indians, Muslim and Hindu alike. Based in Southeast Asia then, I heard for the first time Indian diplomats openly criticizing their government for this act. Under Rajiv Gandhi, democratic India was the first major nation to ban Salman Rushdie's *Satanic Verses*—several months before the Ayatollah Khomeini delivered his death sentence. At about the same time, Gandhi introduced a new defamation bill that would have cut significantly into the freedom of the Indian press. In 1990, out of office and leading the parliamentary opposition, Gandhi threatened to block forcibly a visit to Kashmir or Punjab by Amnesty International to investigate reports of brutal human rights violations in those troubled territories. And this after the partisan machinations of his party had pushed both Punjabi Sikhs and Kashmiri Muslims into radicalism. One searches his record in vain for the sources of the optimism and enthusiasm of his fans.

The dynasty derailed, India now starts over. Many of its problems may seem bigger than those of other democracies, because everything about India is, and some of its crises arise inevitably out of the country's singular cultural environment. But not all the issues consuming India in the 1990s are unrecognizable to us: an inefficent public education system, the sluggish functioning of legislatures, apathy and cynicism about politics (measured in plummeting voter turnout), the demands of linguistic minorities, emotional disputes over affirmative action, discrimination or violence against women, police brutality, and a work ethic that a prominent company director described to *Business India* magazine as "grabbing another person's share of the pie instead of enlarging the pie itself."

Inexplicably, India's political establishment believes it can take on all these demons while trying to hold back the communications revolution. Telephones, roads, and internal air transportation networks rank among the world's worst. A near-religious dislike for computerization rages in some intellectual circles, despite (or perhaps because of) the fact that this is the fastest means of bringing the power of information to the people. With half its people illiterate, there should be a vital role for television. But India's political leaders have turned the national broadcasting monopolies into timid propaganda organs. In a country that would like to rank itself among world powers, television and the press are all but devoid of meaningful international news. Indians relying on their own media would have missed the epochal quality of Tiananmen Square, the collapse of Communism in Eastern Europe, the unification of Germany, the buildup and background to the war in the Persian Gulf, and the disintegration of the Soviet Union, which were at best superficially reported. In urban areas, news-hungry Indians are tapping illegally into Cable News Network signals intended for neighboring countries or watching other international satellite programs New Delhi is powerless to block, while sustaining a unique private news video market within India. Scholars and columnists specializing in international affairs say they have no choice but to rely on costly foreign publications to stay in touch with the world. In a global environment of increasing interaction, India's information vacuum is as dangerous as it is perplexing to its citizens.

"The world has become irrelevant to us," Arun Shourie, one of India's preeminent journalists, wrote recently in *The Economic Times*. "And we have become irrelevant to the world."

In the 1960s, the late Swedish social scientist Gunnar Myrdal produced a monumental, multivolume study of the problems and prospects for development in Asia's new nations, with a special emphasis on India, which he classified as a "soft state." In this exhaustive work, *Asian Drama: An Inquiry into the Poverty of Nations*, Myrdal defined a soft state as one where policies are promulgated but never put into practice, laws are passed but not enforced, glaring inequalities are tolerated by the elite, and there is no social discipline. Without a reasonable level of social discipline, significant development will not take place, he thought. Myrdal, disturbed by a tendency among fellow Western social scientists to escape into euphemism and be too "diplomatic" when confronting the problems of South Asia, made a strong plea for intellectual honesty:

> I am here not arguing against diplomacy, except in scientific research. A scientist should have no other loyalty than to the truth as he perceives it. But apparently to many it is easier to speak boldly in a wealthy country like the United States than to do so in underdeveloped countries. It should be understood that diplomacy of this kind is tantamount to condescension, while to speak frankly is to treat the nationals of these countries as equals. If South Asians realized this, they should be offended by such diplomacy.

This book is about India and the Indians at a terrifying and yet exhilarating moment in their history, a time of daunting problems and tremendous possibilities, a time to throw off old burdens and seize new opportunities in a community of nations being remade geopolitically and economically. The pages that follow are a brief foray into roughly three Indian worlds: the inner, spiritual world rooted in that amorphous creed we label Hinduism; the tangible, real world Indians inhabit and struggle to cope with day to day at the dawn of a new century; and the world outside the unique Indian universe as seen through Indian eyes. Increasingly, these three worlds are impinging on one another. The vibrant myths and powerful talismans that sustain the village clan are making their way into advertising and mass electronic entertainment, even as the trappings of urban middle-class life— laundry detergent, cosmetics, snack foods, plastic pails, and synthetic fabrics—are sold in farming towns. In dealing with the outside world, Indians can display an isolationism intensified by a sense of cultural singularity and superiority that makes some of them seem particularly adversarial in international forums, to which they bring a wealth of original ideas but where they can also be alternately impervious or ultrasensitive to suggestions and criticisms from foreigners. At home, an obsession with preventing Indian civilization and the Indian state from fragmenting under pressure from alienated regional or religious minorities has led to wholesale acts of violence against dissenting communities. Human rights warnings are brushed aside as inapplicable to India, which nonetheless blasts other nations regularly for lesser crimes. It can be a tough country to fathom, but that makes India all the more fascinating.

The writing of this book was undertaken in the spirit of Myrdal's pioneering intellectual journey through Asia. Journalists even more than social scientists should be in the business of discovering and articulating reality without employing mutable standards, however far from home they wander. A reporter in India has especially rich contemporary sources with which to work, and so this book is in large part a glimpse of how India looks at itself. It exists only because hundreds of Indians, from roadside villages to government offices and the independent research organizations with no equals in Asia, were remarkably generous with their time, their ideas, and their observations. Many Indians, writing incisively and speaking frankly about India at this juncture, are quoted in these pages. They can better explain because they better understand their country than any temporary sojourner can.

Indians have another quality that strikes a foreigner working in their midst. We Americans slip quickly into hyperbole and self-hate when criticizing our society's shortcomings. But the Indian intellectual, however trenchant or even vitriolic in criticism of India and the fatal hubris of its leadership, remains a patriot at heart, deeply in love with the country, its cultures, and its unquestioned historical achievements. The sentiment is pervasive. From the village tea stall to the urban think tank, Indians don't want to let their country down. Many, despairing of local and national governments, are taking development and the conservation of what is best in their culture into their own hands, organizing citizens' action groups in cities and small self-help projects in the countryside. In India, this almost always entails personal hardship, and sometimes risk, which they accept willingly. In their commitment may lie India's best hope. Listening to them, you can almost hear the rebound coming.

Indian claim

Cease-fire line   Chinese line of control

Jammu and Kashmir
(Indian Claim)

Himachal
Pradesh

N

0 _____ 300 miles

0 _____ 300 kilometers

30°   30°

Punjab

Arunachal
Pradesh

Haryana

New Delhi

Sikkim

Uttar
Pradesh

Assam   Nagaland

Rajasthan

Meghalaya   Manipur

Ayodhya

Tripura

Bihar

Mizoram

West
Bengal
Calcutta

Gujarat   Madhya
Pradesh

Bhopal

Diu   Daman

20°   20°

Dadra and
Nagar Haveli

Maharashtra

Orissa

Bombay

Hyderabad

Andhra
Pradesh

Pondicherry

Bay of

Goa

Bengal

Arabian

Karnataka

Sea

Bangalore   Madras

Pondicherry

Andaman
and
Nicobar
Islands
(India)

Pondicherry

Tamil
Nadu

Pondicherry

10°   10°

Laccadive
Islands
(India)

Kerala

Trivandrum

70°   80°   90°

I

THE INNER SELF

1

Religion and Myth

For decades if not centuries, India has lured and seduced soul-hungry seekers from the outside world with its intense spirituality and, somewhat paradoxically, the theatricality of its religious rites and symbols. No one who traverses India is untouched by its devotional sense or the brilliance and color of its worship. If there is contemplation, renunciation, and asceticism in its shrines, there is also vigor and noise. The eager clanging of temple bells at nightfall at Ahmedabad's Swaminarayan temple, as the inner sanctum doors open to receive the prayers of frenzied barefoot devotees who race unselfconsciously to prostrate themselves before the gods, can transport the most agnostic Westerner to a new and barely understood universe of belief. It is never unusual to encounter, along a busy commercial road or at a city intersection, a small band of pilgrims holding aloft tinselly homemade constructions destined for a temple, or worshipers all clad in red trekking to their special shrine, or family groups bearing pungent marigold garlands making their way to some personal milestone event. Once crossing the Howrah Bridge over the Hooghly in Calcutta in the morning rush hours, I sat trapped in a taxi caught in a monumental and cacophonous jam as a funeral party, carrying a newly white-wrapped body on a plank, made its way slowly—by foot, and oblivious to the chaos all around—across the river to a cremation ghat. A foreigner need not join a fashionable ashram, or follow an export-model guru, more than a few of them fraudulent, to feel the religiosity of India. The next step is to look at what Indians have made of their spiritual heritage as they struggle to catch up with a fast-developing material world.

Looking for clues to a nation's character in its religious, ethnic, or racial majority may be out of fashion in some places. But in India, where Hinduism in its many forms is woven tightly into the history of the nation, social scientists take a different view. So powerful are the touchstone myths and legends, so pervasive the thought processes rooted in Hinduism, a culture as much as a religion for more than 80 percent of Indians, that from anthropology to political science, in medicine, psychiatry, and the arts, the Hindu context cannot be ignored. Furthermore, with the growth of new or revitalized political and social organizations loosely described as Hindu fundamentalist, the subject of Hinduism and what it means to secular India is back at the center of debate for the first time in half a century. To militant Hindus, the humiliation of centuries of foreign domination by Islamic sultans and emperors and finally imperial Britain can be washed away only by a return to some half-imagined golden age of Hindustan, where history slips into legend and modern borders disappear.

Ancient India is singularly rich in written texts, from the hymns and verses of the *Vedas,* dating to the second millennium B.C., and the later philosophical *Upanishads* and ritual *Brahmanas* to the epic *Mahabharata* (containing the holy *Bhagavad-Gita,* or "Song of the Lord") and the *Ramayana.* But when myth masquerades as chronology, as in the *Puranas* with their catalogue of avatars and dynasties descended from the sun and moon, the old texts open themselves to considerable interpretation. And when other more mundane records have been lost or rewritten to conform to the views of later generations, popular legends fill the gaps, taking the place of history and getting in the way of scholarship. "We Hindus," says K. Natwar Singh, a former government minister and prolific literary critic and essayist, "have a supreme indifference to history. We don't think in linear terms. We think in eternity. The concept of time and space is totally different from the West, and that is why India has not produced a single world-class historian. There is no serious regard for historical authenticity." Any journalist dealing with nationalist religious organizations and government officials knows what he means.

In the *Hindu Contribution to the World of Science,* a booklet given to me by the Vishwa Hindu Parishad, promoter and guardian of the Hindu world view, I read that the "first scientists of the world" were Hindus, the Ashwani Kumar twins, who invented flying cars and hydroplanes about four thousand years ago. Other ancient Hindus, it was asserted, devised atomic theory; pioneered surgery, plastic surgery and the fitting of prostheses; introduced veterinary science and chemistry (finding in the process the formula for extracting gold from mercury). An astronomer named Arya Bhatta proved the earth was round and revolved around the sun; Bhaskaracharya explained gravitation, and Gritsamada introduced the concept of zero. Given the great mathematical skill of contemporary Indians, it is not difficult to entertain the claim (advanced by some scientists elsewhere) that

Hindus invented algebra, geometry, and the decimal system. But the booklet also says that the thinkers of the Subcontinent produced the first alphabet, laid down the theory of evolution, articulated the philosophy of dialectical materialism, and were, inter alia, the first democrats. "The Indians must be regarded as the greatest benefactors of mankind," the treatise concludes.

While ancient Indians are known to have understood the concept of zero, and to have been skilled in surgery on the human body, Hindu nationalists make no effort to place these or other claims in an international context or chronology, beyond using them to challenge the achievements of early Mediterranean, North African, and Near Eastern civilizations. Neighboring China, for example, was also very active in early experimentation and discovery, but little credit goes to important Chinese inventions such as paper, gunpowder, or the compass. Sadly, the unquestioned (if often exaggerated) accomplishments of the Hindu past are thrown up as a defensive smoke screen over present and future national shortcomings. A lot of Indians believe stubbornly that theirs was and therefore still is a unique intellectual universe, and are surprised when the outside world demurs. Mahatma Gandhi thought that something special in Hindu India allowed it to survive when other systems failed. "It has witnessed the fall of Babylonian, Syrian, Persian and Egyptian civilization," he wrote. "Cast a look around you. Where is Rome and where is Greece?"

Myths and legends stay fresh in India. The two most popular television programs of the late 1980s and early 1990s were new serializations of the *Mahabharata*, the epic confrontation between the saintly Pandavas and the duplicitous Kauravas, and of the *Ramayana*, the saga of a god-king wronged. So sacred and real are these stories, even to middle class audiences, that women in affluent Delhi neighborhoods were reported by a newspaper columnist to have taken ritual baths before the weekly screenings. In *The Great Indian Novel*, one of the best and most original works of fiction to appear in India in recent years, the author Shashi Tharoor cleverly utilizes the *Mahabharata* form to lampoon contemporary politics and society. "Whatever our ancestors expected of India, Ganipati, it was not this," says Ved Vyas, the chronicler, to his godly scribe in Tharoor's book. "It was not a land where *dharma* and duty have come to mean nothing, where religion is an excuse for conflict rather than a code of conduct; where piety, instead of marking wisdom, masks a crippling lack of imagination. It was not a land where brides are burned in kerosene-soaked kitchens because they have not brought enough dowry with them; where integrity and self respect are for sale to the highest bidder; where men are pulled off buses and butchered because of the length of a forelock or the absence of a foreskin."

Tharoor says he chose this recasting of an epic as a vehicle for his work because the *Mahabharata* has a popular relevance and significance throughout India. "You constantly hear people referred to in terms of characters in the *Mahabharata*, or episodes in the *Mahabharata*, because it's a story that many people have sought to find relevance in throughout the changing times. I felt, too, that the *Mahabharata* both reflects and contributes to the public consciousness of the nation. It's almost a ready-made model for an historical saga, which at the same time tries to encapsulate some of the principles, values, issues, and concerns of the society. So I said to myself, What would a twenty-ninth-century Ved Vyas tell us about his India if he were writing about the twentieth century?"

The psychoanalyst Sudhir Kakar, who in the early 1980s wrote a ground-breaking study of the Hindu mind, *The Inner World: A Psychoanalytic Study of Childhood and Society in India,* says that "the role of myths, especially those of religious derivation, in defining and integrating the traditional elements and the common features of identity and society in Hindu India—certainly in the past, and in most parts of the community till today—cannot be over-estimated." In the *Mahabharata,* for example, there is Kunti, the supermom who could "gracefully define her sons' thoughts and spare them the awk-wardness of expressing them"—a precursor of the dominating, suffocating Indian mother-cum-mother-in-law of today. The epic has violence, gore, revenge, cunning, and trickery—staples of the current Hindi cinema. There is envy, now a common advertising strategy. There are curses that can never be undone, only modified through "boons." In a tight spot, the trick is to assume a pose of supplication to authority and beg for the grant of a boon, a mitigating favor (perhaps with a bit of good magic). By this logic, the modern-day police superintendent who allows riotous mobs to run amok for three or four days in his city avoids disciplinary action or dismissal by secur-ing a transfer.

To be born a Hindu in contemporary democratic India is to be thrust into a thicket of conflicts. Growing up in the most individualistic of religions, taught to seek his or her own salvation through any one or more of a pan-theon of gods and their avatars and a panoply of forms and rituals, little Kumar or Madhu is at the same time trapped in a web of family relation-ships and duties. These can limit social and intellectual freedom, atrophy an analytical mind, and curtail the development of a wider civic culture by encouraging commitment and loyalty only to the extended family, clan, or caste. At the upper levels of caste, this fosters social Darwinism, as was demonstrated in the violent protests against affirmative action that helped bring down the government of Vishwanath Pratap Singh in 1990. "If the Harijans haven't made anything of themselves by now," a journalist in Delhi remarked of India's untouchables, who are already the beneficiaries of a government quota system, "then they mustn't have what it takes." At the bottom of the social order, the glass ceilings and walls of caste breed despair, frustration, and, increasingly, violence.

In Hindu India social behavior may be dictated less by the spirit of Hin-duism and more by its literature—Kakar's "dense, defiant overgrowth of myths." The messages and role models contained in these epics and legends often run counter to modernizing social trends, especially where women are concerned. In the Hindu home, particularly if it is upper caste, the rules of ritual purity may be strict, but concepts of order and cleanliness do not necessarily extend to the world beyond the gate. A Brahmin professor in Calcutta now campaigning for better city amenities explained this by recalling how his mother had nagged him relentlessly as a child about emptying his bowels and washing his body at daybreak, but thought nothing of servants throwing all the household rubbish out into the street. Indian hospitals are notorious for their inattention to sanitation, not to mention comfort. Public buildings are not cleaned or maintained; the corridors leading to the offices of India's government spokesmen reek of urine and are stained with *paan* juice spit into corners or in the general direction of receptacles.

In the drab northern city of Patna, another Brahmin and a social scientist, Bindeshwar Pathak, has given more than two decades of his life to attacking a central taboo separating Hindus with caste from the untouchables: the handling of human excrement. Through his grassroots sanitation service, Sulabh International, he leads a crusade to end scavenging, which in Indian terms is most narrowly defined as the carrying away of human waste in a country where tens of millions of homes still lack rudimentary latrines. While building public toilets across India and arranging vocational education for scavengers, Pathak also marches outcastes into temples normally reserved for the upper castes and invites them to dine with the Brahmin priest-teachers known as pandits, acts that could cost him his life. Caste discrimination, from separate (but never equal) temples to separate polling booths on election day, is a fact of life in India, especially but not exclusively in North India, where social rules are often enforced with lynch-mob violence. In August 1991, a lower-caste policeman took shelter from the monsoon rain in an upper-caste temple in a village in the western state of Maharashtra and was stoned and kicked to death by the Brahmins whose singing of devotional songs he had interrupted.

Hindu India, with its many divisions, lacks a sense of community—or, as a Southeast Asian diplomat once remarked to me, "It's a country with a lot of spirituality but very little charity." This theme inevitably surfaces in the social critiques made by Indians who are not Hindus, but it is not limited to them, as Pathak demonstrates. Hindu reformers over more than two centuries have preached and written about the dearth of community spirit; today's civic-action and environmental lobbies, consumer organizations, and secular political parties wrestle with the problem. So, in a sense, do some internationally known gurus, ashrams, and movements practicing group worship if not social action. M. S. S. Nambudiri, director of a vocational school and home for orphans run by the Seva Samajan service organization in Madras, remarked how Nehru had spoken often of the need for more community spirit to speed development, "but the truth is that we live in a society of maximum conflict in caste, class, and politics." It is the strategy of Hindu militants to create a sense of community by welding Hinduism to Indian nationalism. Unfortunately, they would also abolish the concept of minority rights in the process.

Leela Rao, professor of film at Bangalore University (and a Brahmin) argues that in Hinduism "the focus is on self, but without selfishness," suggesting that there is no deliberate or premeditated rejection of a social conscience. Its development is simply not considered part of religion, she said in a conversation in her small office on a shady, shabby campus in India's most cosmopolitan city. "Hindu philosophy is so much self-oriented; in practical terms, you go to the temple only as a means to your own salvation. The universe is one, and you must find yourself and become a part of that universe. In this search, no one can do anything for you and you can't do anything for anybody else. Spiritual salvation is never for the community." The late Kshiti Mohan Sen, a linguist and founder with Rabindranath Tagore of the university and scholarly retreat at Shantiniketan, pointed out that Indian languages had developed no exact synonyms for the word "charity."

Hinduism has no rule-giving hierarchy or theological seminaries debating doctrine in a changing world as we know these institutions in the West. The historian Romila Thapar thinks the term "Hinduism" was itself a generic term invented by outsiders and probably not even used widely until the eighth century A.D., when Arabs needed a name for Indian worship, mostly of Shiva and Vishnu, two gods who, with Brahma, form a Hindu trinity. Later European scholars and Orientalists picked up the usage. Hinduism was not founded by a historical person or handed down to earth by revelation. Though rich in treatises and epics, Hinduism, which evolved from and still remains divided into many sects and cults, has no single holy book by which humankind could strive to live; no Bible, no Quran, no Confucian manual of right behavior. There are no Ten Commandments. There is no heaven and hell. Lacking a uniform, agreed code of ethics, Hinduism cannot easily offer a grassroots alternative to the essentially British legal system India inherited at independence, a system some would argue is inherently Judeo-Christian and therefore alien, despite the addition of family laws for the nation's major religious groups. As corruption mounts in an age of growing scarcity and materialism, there are no automatic theological brakes on lawlessness. Prime Minister Chandra Shekhar, who coincidentally had the briefest tenure of any head of government (four months in 1990–91, plus another four as caretaker), liked to tell reporters that it really didn't matter too much if politicians took bribes. India had bigger problems of poverty, illiteracy, and disease, he said. But many of those bigger problems were being exacerbated by corrupt legislators and bureaucrats siphoning off funds for development in one of the biggest pork-barreling arenas on the planet. There are no institutions of accountability that politicians have not proved they can overrule or ignore. Interestingly, some Hindu militants are now calling for a more organized response from sages and gurus to moral waywardness and the excesses of caste. Anandshankar Padya, a Bombay writer, suggests in an essay published by the Vishwa Hindu Parishad that it is time Hindu leaders "put their heads together and evolved a concise, modern, scientific religious code based on the basic tenets of Hinduism."

The ancient treatises, beginning with the 2,200–year-old law code of Manu and subsequent commentaries on it, are ample lodes to be mined. These appeal to nationalistic Hindus who would force the secular nation into conformity with its majority religion. Such voices are heard from within the membership of the largely cultural Vishwa Hindu Parishad, the Bharatiya Janata political party, and the Rashtriya Swayamsevak Sangh, with its squads of highly disciplined militants whom many Indians regard as protofascist storm troopers of the faith. But much of Hindu India's legal literature—most of all the *Manu Smrti*, or *Lawbook of Manu*—provokes fierce controversy among other Indians because of its institutionalization of caste and other socially retrogressive behavior. In an age of equality, the Manu code is unacceptably male chauvinist on the role of women. "Her father protects her in childhood, her husband protects her in youth, her sons protect her in old age—a woman does not deserve independence," it says. If women are permitted to run around unguarded, it adds, "they would bring grief to both the families." Ainslie Embree, a lifelong scholar and friend of India who recently retired as professor of history and director of Columbia University's Southern Asian Institute, says that in modern India "no one, not even the BJP or the RSS, would argue for the code of Manu now, but the RSS would say that we have to restate those ideals."

Among the more troublesome and now-indefensible practices codified by Manu was the strict division of Hindu society into four *varnas*, or categories (the word means "colors") of caste, which are then again divided into many subcastes or *jatis*. Manu assigned scholarly and ritual functions to the highest *varna*, the Brahmins, a small minority of Indians then and now. For the warrior Kshatriyas, next in rank, the code listed protection of the people and some ceremonial functions. The Vaishyas, third of the *varnas*, were expected to be traders, merchants, moneylenders, and farmers. For the Shudras, there was only one task: to serve the three higher orders. Outcastes were and are outside the system entirely. It is a matter of intense controversy in India whether using castes and subcastes to determine which groups are eligible for affirmative action is not in fact reinforcing a social system the Nehru generation thought it could abolish by law.

It is arguable that any Hindu-based legal code intended for universal application would be difficult to formulate, as Sudhir Kakar suggests in his psychoanalysis of the Indian mind, in which he notes that right and wrong are relative not absolute concepts in Hindu tradition. "Hindu philosophy and ethics teach that right action for an individual depends on *desa*, the culture in which he is born; on *kala*, the period of historical time in which he lives; on *srama*, the efforts required of him at different stages of life; and on *gunas*, the innate psychological traits which are the heritage of an individual's previous lives. In lessening the burden of individual responsibility for action, Hindu culture at the same time alleviates the pain of guilt suffered in other societies by those whose (real or fancied) actions transgress rigid thou-shalt and thou-shalt-not axioms."

When the Educational Testing Service in Princeton discovered in late 1989 that its standardized tests were being sold widely in India in advance of examination dates—the biggest case of fraud the service has ever faced—I spoke with the head of the Indian foundation designated as the testing service's agent in India. He was unfazed. Security was not his problem, he said. But weren't the sealed test packets entrusted to him? Yes, but it was not his job to find out what happened to them when they left his office. Two years later, New Delhi was shocked by widespread reports of open cheating on a standardized secondary school–leaving examination. Newspapers wrote about and photographed friends and relatives coming to school fences to hand over answers to questions. Not long after, it was discovered that test papers for the Indian civil service examinations, the key to the best jobs in government, were being sold openly on the Delhi University campus. In cases such as these, cheaters and their accomplices—not infrequently teachers or administrators who accept bribes—argue confidently that the importance of doing well in these exams overrides other considerations. In the July 1992 edition of the monthly video documentary *Newstrack*, young people were not ashamed to say this to the camera. Poor students who study hard and long because they cannot afford to pay black-market prices for civil service test papers are heartbroken when these examinations, or parts of them, have to be annulled. For some, there will be no second chance; their families put all their resources into one shot at a lifelong sinecure. The knowledge that money can buy just about anything eats away at the determination of the disadvantaged. They don't, for example, have the $2,500 needed to buy a bogus University of California degree, which UCLA found advertised in Indian newspapers recently. The fake degrees seemed to be circulating only in India, where credentials are often not checked, particularly if a small consideration is paid to the responsible official.

More than twenty years before independence in 1947, Sarvepalli Radhakrishnan, India's best-known twentieth-century philosopher and president of the country from 1962 to 1967, worried about the modern misuse or misunderstanding of a religion in which "intellect is subordinated to intuition," and society is tolerant and permissive to a fault. "The law of karma encourages the sinner that it is never too late to mend," he wrote in *The Hindu View of Life*, based on a series of lectures delivered at Oxford University. Karma, a complex concept for the uninitiated, roughly comprises the accumulated influences and deeds of earlier lives that a reincarnated Hindu carries with him or her and strives eventually to improve or lose in a future rebirth. "It persuades us to adopt a charitable view towards the sinner, for men are more often weak than vicious." But, Radhakrishnan added: "Unfortunately, the theory of karma became confused with fatality in India when man himself grew feeble and was disinclined to do his best. It was made into an excuse for inertia and timidity and was turned into a message of despair and not hope."

Nearly three-quarters of a century later, *The Tribune* newspaper of Chandigarh raised similar themes in castigating Punjab University for allowing three years to elapse before punishing a faculty scientist who had published and displayed fraudulent "proof" that he had found hitherto unseen fossils in the high Himalayas—mostly in strategic regions conveniently barred to foreigners by the Indian government. After his bluff was called by a scientist at an Australian university, Punjab hunkered down and stayed hunkered even when the Geological Survey of India concluded that the fossils were fakes. Some had apparently been bought in shops abroad. This "demeaning controversy," *The Tribune* warned, was damaging the reputations of all the institution's scholars. The professor was eventually dismissed. The example has stuck in the minds of foreign scientists, however. A World Bank expert told me later that international organizations are often skeptical of scientific findings from Indian universities, a tragic problem for the many Indian researchers whose work is unquestionably honest.

Karma or not, the tendency toward moral relativism and a concurrent Hindu disinclination to take a rigorous individual stand on issues can lead to an unnecessary lack of self-confidence at national level for a country of this size. India often produces muddled responses to international issues, as intense national pride and a sense of manifest destiny collide with an unwillingness to make bold policy moves. Wild allegations and abstractions are hurled around and sanctimonious speeches made, but concrete proposals or rational analyses rarely follow. Prime Minister Chandra Shekhar thought that an institutionalized inferiority complex had reduced the Indian foreign service to a den of weasels during the 1990–1991 Persian Gulf crisis, throughout which India was never able to articulate a strong public policy and act on it. Every initiative the prime minister undertook to align New Delhi with United Nations resolutions prompted a scampering of foreign affairs specialists to Shekhar's corner of South Block (the palatial building at the crest of Raj Path that the prime minister and the Ministry of External Affairs share) with warnings of dire political, diplomatic, or strategic consequences.

"If you fail to take a decision at a crucial moment, you don't only fail for that moment, but you fail for decades, you fail the nation itself," Shekhar told me after the war ended and he had endured a storm of criticism for allowing Gulf-bound American transport planes to refuel in India. A. P. Venkataswaran, a former foreign secretary, went farther in saying in a newspaper column at about the same time that the highly developed Indian skills of sycophancy and flattery were in fact manifestations of weak knees; he quoted Mahatma Gandhi's remark that cowardice was a greater Indian problem than poverty. A few months later, when scandals began to unravel at the Bank of Credit and Commerce International, the first response of a new government under P. V. Narasimha Rao, Rajiv Gandhi's successor as Congress Party leader, was to rule out a Parliamentary committee investigation of BCCI's Bombay branch. Arab nations might be offended. Prominent Indians might also have been exposed.

Psycho-political analyses suggest that there is also much in Hinduism and its myths to reinforce a very personalized dependent behavior, with the focus of dependency always mutable according to circumstances. In the *Mahabharata* there is a wonderful episode in which a king called Salya, hearing that the great war between the Pandavas (good) and Kauravas (evil) is about to begin, raises a huge army and sets off to cast his lot with the Pandavas. En route to the battle, he passes through the territory of Duryodhana, the Kaurava chief. Duryodhana, a master of trickery, quickly erects comfortable resthouses of "wondrous hospitality" in the path of Salya's advancing army. Salya is delighted, and so impressed with what he takes to be the chivalry of Duryodhana that he promptly switches sides. He feels very sorry a little later, but explains to the stunned Pandavas that "no one can prevent or alter what has been ordained by fate." Cut to 1989 and 1990 and the Delhi hotel suites where members of Parliament are wined and dined before being bought and sold.

Paradoxes abound in permissive, tolerant Hindu India (proving again, as every foreigner is frequently told, that whatever you say about the country, the opposite is probably also true). At some temples, non-Hindus are turned away brusquely by outraged guardians to be fleeced by accomplices with "viewing platforms" outside the walls; at others they are welcomed. The Hindu religion, still more of a collection of sects and individual beliefs than a single faith, can bar devotees of the "wrong" caste or no caste at all from a shrine, yet does have the capacity to make room for everybody somewhere. At the Bechraji temple, about fifty miles west of Ahmedabad in Gujarat state, a community of eunuchs and transvestites dominates a corner of the sacred compound, asking for donations in return for gratuitous "blessings," just as they do before festival seasons in central Delhi office buildings, where areas of turf have been established. The same group always called on us, and were welcomed as old acquaintances by P. J. Anthony, the veteran office manager of *The New York Times*, who possessed an encyclopedic knowledge of Indian quirks and customs and had developed a hundred ploys to prevent naive correspondents from falling into traps. Many people fear transvestites, however, because of lurid rumors that they steal baby boys for castration or are capable of conjuring up curses.

Bechraji is a center for the worship of the Bahuchara Mata or Mataji, a form of the goddess Durga. Legend says that when a patrol of Muslim soldiers passed this way once upon a time in the dim past, they ate some sacred fowl. Mataji caused their stomachs to be torn open by the roosters they had devoured. Graphic folk art paintings of this event can be found on the walls of a number of temples in the vicinity. The eunuchs at Bechraji, who worship the goddess, are hostile to prying outsiders. Their unofficial leader, whom they called "the boss," threatened to chase me away with blows until a sympathetic temple priest intervened, and drew one or two of the group into conversation. As the pandit spoke, my understanding of their plight and their attachment to the temple grew. The eunuchs were not all true eunuchs, or *hijras*, said Pandit Umiya Shankar Joshi. Some were homosexuals, cross-dressers (he did not use the phrase but only spoke of the concept), impotent men, or others unhappy for various reasons in the married life into which virtually all Indians are forced by family pressure. Some were old men who had left their homes and chosen to come here to spend their declining years gathering grace, as others might go to a place of pilgrimage in the hills and take on the robes of a mendicant. The temple gives this little peripheral community a base and a purpose, with no one making judgments about choices of lifestyle or sexual preferences. Some of the "women" (all wearing saris, makeup, and jewels) had become very prosperous taking money from people afraid of a *hijra* curse, bystanders said, gathering as Indians so willingly do to join in proffering advice. But nobody around the temple square could recall a castration or other act of violence against a child. Indeed, boys are brought here for a ceremonial (possibly symbolic) haircut, a visit recorded for the family album by photographers who stroll the temple grounds in search of business. Vendors sell toys at the gate.

Most modern Hindus, heirs to a culture that produced an extraordinary amount of erotic art and made worship of the *Shiva lingam*, a phallus, central to the spiritual life of millions, paradoxically inhabit an environment of extreme prudery and strict social convention, hardly less inhibiting than that of their Muslim neighbors, many of whom still keep their women in purdah or at least out of mixed company. Added to a system of loveless arranged marriages and an unimaginable absence of knowledge about human sexuality in anything but a very superficial sense—a subject almost never written about in an instructive way in the press—tensions build. Now and then frustrations explode into uniquely Indian riots as, for example, at film festivals when foreign movies, permitted more license in matters of passion and sex than their censored Indian counterparts, fail to deliver on their rumored salaciousness. Movie theaters have been sacked by outraged mobs of Indian boys and men baying for lust. In 1991, audiences walked out wholesale on special screenings of *Sex, Lies and Videotape* after realizing they had been more than a little misled by the title. Each spring, during the festival of Holi, once a joyous romp in which men and women throw colored powders and water at one another in fun, women now hide from men who prowl campuses and residential neighborhoods bent on a clumsy grope, or worse. When India's most publicized sexologist organized the country's first international conference on orgasm in 1991—at a respectable New Delhi hotel—uniformed guards had to be posted at the door of an accompanying exhibition on sex in Indian art. Both the decision to put on the show of high-brow pornography and the craze to see it were inexplicable. There is better stuff in the National Museum, or in any number of sculpture-filled caves.

A touching first-person account of the agony of youth in this restricted society outside the circles in which foreigners tend to move was published in a letter that the magazine *The Week* highlighted in its issue of July 1, 1990. A young man (his photograph indicated he may have been in his early twenties), J. Satya Narayan Murty, from Khagual, in the poor and often violent state of Bihar, wrote:

> I kissed my girlfriend in a public place with her consent. The people who were around at once stared at us as if we had committed a big crime. It was no doubt a very strange sight to them. My girlfriend, for an instant, felt shy, but soon put on a bold face. I was proud of her. The kiss became hot news among the locals. And my girlfriend's parents, who heard about it, summoned me. I went and faced their anger. In their opinion, I was guilty and so they wanted me to apologize. I justified myself by saying that I had done nothing against her wishes—it was a frank expression of our spontaneous feelings. As we expected, her so-called well-wishers put pressure on her not to meet me again. And she succumbed to it. After all, she is an Indian girl. I am not unfamiliar with our social mores. But I strongly justify free and frank expression of desires and feelings, provided that they are not unfair and lead to no harm. And I do believe that a kiss is the best expression of love, and it is not an unfair act as long as it is not forced on anyone. No doubt, we are developing. But developing materially, not mentally. Moreover, our mentality is degenerating with the passage of time. A boy-girl relationship is always looked on with suspicion. Boys and girls are treated like different species. The gap is very wide, and our so-called traditional society ensures that this remains so. Even now, in most families, girls are not free to choose their life partners. I believe this is one of the reasons why many social crimes occur in our country. A caged lion is more violent than a free one.

2

Women and Minorities

INDIAN WOMEN, who suffer both sexual frustration and the humiliation of abuse in intimate relations, a subject I will return to later in this book,
are routinely told that they live on pedestals, adored as goddesses by men.
Psychiatrists and women's rights activists say otherwise—that most young
women merely bear up until they can gain stature by producing a son—but
the fantasy persists. In a public speech in November 1990, the chief justice
of the Supreme Court of India, Ranganath Mishra, allowed that he did not
really agree with the constitutional provision giving women legal equality.
He thought the trend should be away from jobs and back into the home,
where they could make life for their families "a heaven on earth." A
woman, he said, "is a deity to be worshipped" who should "fight for her
superior status." Only a few newspaper columnists and editorial writers
questioned the propriety of the chief justice opposing both the constitution
and the rights of women in general. Angry women protested, but could not
turn this into an issue of public importance in a society that obviously did
not see it as a problem. A few months later, a Russian woman living in New
Delhi with her journalist husband wandered into this atmosphere by accident when she accepted an invitation to address a service club lunch on the
subject of women in what was then the Soviet Union. She talked of
women's rights, divorce, a liberal attitude toward sex, and wide opportunities for careers and employment, drawing a few implicit and explicit comparisons with the inhibited lives of Indian women without being too
provocative, she thought. She was interrupted by affronted Indians. "We
treat our women like goddesses here!" one shouted. "Indian women are

much better off than women in other countries!" She was still talking about the experience a few weeks later. "I told them, I came here to give you information, not to start a revolution. I couldn't believe the reaction."

In the vast majority of Indian homes, a woman is expected to grow up chaste in an extended family where uncles, cousins, and in-laws may be tempted to abuse her sexually from an early age. A social worker in New Delhi, who is trying to help unmarried pregnant teenagers bear healthy children for adoption by other Indians rather than abandon them to the sea of street urchins or to foreign homes, said that the first hurdle in her job is convincing a middle class family to face the truth, accept that the fault was probably not the girl's, and avoid the instinctive urge to ostracize the victim.

There is, not surprisingly, a mythological precedent for this tendency to attach guilt to a woman before the facts are in. It can be found in the story of Sita, the role model for Indian girls. Sita was the consort of Rama, a personification of Vishnu and the hero of the *Ramayana* who as a prince was deprived of his royal inheritance and driven from the kingdom by the connivance of his half-brother Bharata, Bharata's mother, Kaikeyi, and her maid, Manthara. Sent into exile in the wilderness for fourteen years, Rama tries to dissuade Sita (and another half-brother, Lakshmana) from following him into a life of rustic hardship. But Sita—according to my schoolchild's version of the story—assures her lord that "with you by my side, thorns would feel like flowers." For her pains, she then gets abducted from her forest hut by the ogre of the age, Ravana, the demon-king of Lanka. Pure to the core, she resists all his blandishments and is eventually released by Hanuman, the monkey god, and his simian army. Is Rama happy to have her back? Not entirely. What if she is not telling the truth about what went on in Lanka? She walks through fire to prove her innocence. In the end, even that is not enough. Back in Ayodhya, his throne restored, King Rama hears about new rumors circulating the palace about Sita's faithlessness. Facing judgment by the mob, heartbroken Sita asks Mother Earth to swallow her. A fissure opens and down she goes. At that point—according to another version of the story written for young minds and sold at Mahatma Gandhi's Sabarmati ashram in Gujarat—the sage Valmiki consoles the startled Rama thus: "Sita was the daughter of the earth. The earth has taken back her loving daughter. What is done can't be undone. Sita won't come back. It is not wise to cry over her." The people of Ayodhya cheer Rama and his sons, and life goes on.

India's minority religious communities—Muslims, Christians, Buddhists, Sikhs, Jains, Parsis, and Jews; nearly all faiths with a more developed community spirit and higher levels of collective social action—react in differing ways and degrees to life within the dominant Hindu culture. Religious freedom is guaranteed by India's constitution and there are no laws against conversion, although foreign missionaries are sometimes deported and always discouraged from coming to India, where Hindu militants would like to restrict the activities of all proselytizers. Relations between religious groups also vary from one part of the country to another. In the South, where Christianity has been part of the spiritual landscape since the first century and Hindu revivalism is not so strong as in the North, there have been many efforts by Christian groups to "Indianize" the languages and rituals of religion, bringing in customs that are associated with Hindu worship: the use of lamps, incense, and Indian music, or the construction of less traditional churches where worshipers sit on the floor, not in pews. In Bombay, Father Francis Barboza, a priest of the Roman Catholic Society of the Divine Word, has brought classical South Indian dances into his ministry, giving a distinctive Indian theatricality to acts of devotion.

Christianity, despite its teachings about the brotherhood of humankind, has not been able to shake the stigma of caste in India, where sharp social distinctions separate converts, often known as "Indian Christians," especially in North India, from upper caste Christian communities more numerous in the South, on the Portuguese-influenced west coast, and around Calcutta. Nirad C. Chaudhuri, whose acidic books on Indian society are written from his English home in Oxford (as Indians are quick to point out), tells a story in one of his works, *The Continent of Circe*, about an encounter he had with a woman from the western city of Mangalore. Chaudhuri made the mistake of describing her as an Indian Christian. She shot back: "I am not an Indian Christian. I am a Catholic. Indian Christians are low-caste converts to Protestantism." Chaudhuri, a Bengali, remembered how Calcutta Christians with names like Banerji, Chatterji, Mukherji, Bose, or Dutt would keep their distance from Christians named Biswas. When the son of a prominent Calcutta Christian wanted to marry a woman with a low-caste family name, Chaudhuri recalled, "the father at first strongly objected and his sister told us: 'After all, we are Brahmins.' "

Many Christians are troubled that while they believe their religion is as Indian as any other, they are always open to the suspicion of being somehow "Westernized" because of their faith. With upwards of 60 percent of India's Christians listed as converts or the descendants of converts from Hinduism, militant Hindus regard re-conversion as a duty. Another target group for zealots—who consider most citizens of the Subcontinent as Hindus, lapsed Hindus, or potential Hindus—are the Buddhists, many of whom left the Hindu world in an (often fruitless) effort to erase untouchability, following the example of Bhimrao Ramji Ambedkar, the legal scholar who headed the committee that wrote India's constitution. Born an untouchable of the lowly Mahar community, Ambedkar never ceased despairing of Hinduism's inability to create an egalitarian or even equitable society. His own professional achievements in life, made possible by the patronage of an enlightened maharaja and scholarships that took him to Columbia University, the London School of Economics, and Gray's Inn, were an exception to the rule. In 1951, he resigned as law minister over differences with Nehru and the Congress Party on caste discrimination in independent India. In 1956, not long before he died, he became a Buddhist.

There is historical precedent for his conversion also. The Emperor Ashoka of the ancient Maurya dynasty, who reigned from 268 to 233 B.C., became a Buddhist out of revulsion for the excesses of his own imperial power, apparently after conquering the smaller kingdom of Kalinga in eastern India (now Orissa state) with a huge loss of life on both sides. "Even if the number of those killed and captured in the conquest of Kalinga had been a hundred or a thousand times less, it would be grievous," he wrote in one of his post-conversion edicts carved on rock pillars and posted at various points in his empire. The rock edicts instruct all people in the basic virtues of self-control and humane behavior toward others. "I have had this inscription of righteousness engraved that all my sons and grandsons may not seek to gain new victories, that in whatever victories they may gain they may prefer forgiveness and light punishment, that they may consider the only victory the victory of righteousness." Ashoka has become a figure of veneration throughout the Asian Buddhist world, in which India, once the cradle of Buddhism, now plays a negligible part.

Building a modern working relationship with the Hindu majority and the often upper-caste-dominated institutions of the the Indian state is most difficult for more than 100 million Indian Muslims. Some disadvantages are historical, political, and economic, growing out of the 1947 Partition of British India and the creation of Muslim Pakistan. In strictly religious terms, however, most Muslims on the Subcontinent are constrained by inflexible articles of faith and practice that do not allow the kind of compromises Christian churches can make in forms and settings for worship. Although mystic Sufism had influence on pockets of Islam, in most parts of India a generally conservative Muslim clergy has demonstrated scant conciliatory liberalism or imagination in recent years. Furthermore, many Hindus are unsettled by Islam's cosmopolitan ideal, its sense of a brotherhood of nations and believers circling the world (or somehow encircling India) with a common faith. Muhammad Iqbal, the poet and philosopher of Subcontinental Islam who is revered in both India and Pakistan, expressed this in a verse:

> Our Essence is not bound to any place;
> The vigor of our wine is not contained
> In any bowl; Chinese and Indian
> Alike the shard that constitutes our jar,
> Turkish and Syrian alike the clay
> Forming our body. . . .

Islam does not separate religion and the state, a concept that has bedeviled integration not only in South Asia but also in Southeast Asia, particularly in Indonesia, with its 90 percent Muslim majority, the largest Islamic community in the world, chafing under or at best enduring an official "national religion," Pancasila. In India, Hindu fundamentalists often understand better than other Indians the Muslim concept of a unitary state defined by religion because of their dream of an openly Hindu nation, which they insist would be more tolerant than its Islamic counterpart since that is the nature of Hinduism. But talk of a Hindu nation only heightens the apprehensions and sense of vulnerability among Indian Muslims, many of whom have been victimized by Hindus in the secular state they now inhabit. Mohammed Aslam, a scholar of Muslim politics in India, reflected a growing sense of anger and frustration among Muslim intellectuals when he described in *The State, Political Processes and Identity*, a 1989 collection of essays by various authors, the climate in which millions of Muslims live in Uttar Pradesh, India's most populous state and a traditional center of Subcontinental Islam. In Uttar Pradesh, where Hindu-Muslim clashes (or attacks on Muslim neighborhoods) are frequent, the Provincial Armed Constabulary, or PAC, is more or less regarded by many Muslims as a Hindu army rather than a state police force. "The trend in Uttar Pradesh now," says Aslam, "is that whenever there is communal tension leading to minor altercations (almost ever-present in the prevailing environment), the PAC is moved in to disperse the more volatile elements of the two communities, curfew is imposed, and the PAC is let loose on the Muslims like a pack of hounds hunting hares."

At Aligarh Muslim University, Abida Samauddin, a political scientist, scrutinized reporting in several Hindi-language newspapers in North India during the violence surrounding the 1990 attack on the Babri Masjid, the sixteenth-century mosque in Ayodhya militant Hindus claim as the birthplace of Rama. She found much of what was printed unreliable or concocted and dangerously provocative in its bias toward Hindu militancy. In a conversation early the following January in her sunny garden, an oasis in a city still recovering from Hindu-Muslim rioting, she described India's Muslims as silent spectators to the rise of political fascism in the guise of religion. Reflecting Muslim skepticism over legislation to protect all places of worship (except the Babri Masjid, a special case), she said that "today it is one mosque, tomorrow another—they have a list of 3,000." Azra Razzack, a research scholar at Delhi University's Department of Education, made a study of Muslim stereotypes in Indian textbooks and classroom lessons, and concluded that most portrayals showed an intolerant, violent people—usually in some kind of distinguishing costume—who are basically "antinational." In one case, a teacher had been telling children (perhaps out of ignorance more than anything else) that Muslims did not eat pork because the pig was sacred to them.

The extraordinary accomplishments of Muslims—builders of the Taj Mahal and scores of palaces, weavers, landscape designers, and painters of great skill—are often undervalued by Hindu India, whose temple architects, lacking the arch and dome, built dark, massive towers often distinguished only by their sculpture and friezes. When Doordarshan, India's government-run national television network, showed a controversial serialization of the historical novel *The Sword of Tipu Sultan*, based on the life of an Islamic hero who fought the British to his death in South India in the eighteenth century, each segment was preceded by a disclaimer saying in effect that not everything in the film was necessarily true. Hindus had complained that the book, written by a Hindu author, Bhagwan S. Gidwani, was too flattering to the protagonist. The series attracted a huge audience nonetheless: ordinary Indians, almost always more sensible and less thin-skinned than their leaders, love a good tale.

Khushwant Singh, a historian of the Sikh religion as well as a journalist and novelist, now in his seventies, acknowledges that a pervasive prejudice against Muslims marked the Punjab of his boyhood, a state that was to suffer most in the bloody Partition of British India into Hindu-majority and Muslim nations in 1947. In conversations, Singh also mourns the increasing ghettoization of his own Sikh people since 1984, especially in New Delhi, where several thousand innocent people died and millions of dollars worth of property was destroyed in the politically motivated attacks on Sikh neighborhoods after the assassination of Indira Gandhi by Sikh bodyguards. During and after the 1984 attacks many Sikhs returned to a stricter observance of the rules of their faith, with older members of the community saying that for the first time they no longer felt a spiritual kinship with Hindus. The shock was also felt by Sikhs living abroad. Gurcharan Singh, now an American citizen who teaches international relations at Marymount Manhattan College, said that 1984 completely reversed his drift into secularism. He gave up alcohol and resumed saying his daily prayers. He has also become active in overseas campaigns on behalf of Indian Sikhs suffering human rights abuses. Many Sikhs abroad have moved into open support for the independence of Punjab, a Sikh nation they would call Khalistan.

In a 1991 collection of essays, *Need for a New Religion in India*, Khushwant Singh, who is firmly opposed to the Khalistani Sikh independence campaign, deplores what he interprets as a general surfeit of Indian religiosity in these difficult times. "It can scarcely be disputed that we Indians, be we Hindus, Muslims, Christians, Sikhs, or Parsis, spend more time in performing religious rituals than any other people in the world," he wrote. "Count the number of religious holidays, national and sectional, then add up the number of hours people spend every day in saying their prayers, visiting temples, mosques, churches, and gurudwaras; the days spent in pilgrimage to holy places; the hours taken up by *satsangs, pravachans, keertans, bhajans,* etc. It will come to a staggering total. Then ask yourself whether a poor developing country like ours can afford to lose so many millions of man hours in pursuits which produce no material benefits?"

Here Khushwant Singh, India's best-known gadfly and humorist (both small intellectual professions in a country that tends to take itself very seriously), runs counter to the Gandhian myth of anti-materialism and antipathy toward Western concepts of "progress." Such views still motivate Indian thinking in diverse quarters, creating, among other phenomena, an anti-development lobby among intellectuals. Mahatma Gandhi once wrote to a seeker that he was "not enamoured" of Western material progress. "In fact, it almost seems as though God in his wisdom had prevented India from progressing along those lines so that it might fulfill its special mission of resisting the onrush of materialism," he said.

Paulos Mar Gregorios, the American-educated Metropolitan in Delhi of the Eastern Orthodox Syrian Church, is a contemporary critic of Western philosophical concepts of progress and their concurrent theories of development. This has led him into the diverse school of revisionists who question whether Nehru was too much influenced by foreign liberals, eager to throw away the past when it got in the way of the future. In *Enlightenment: East and West,* published in 1989, Gregorios suggested that Nehru was ignorant of the complexity of Indian life, with its deep roots in a subconsciously powerful cultural history. He scorns Nehru for calling for a break with tradition. "The past may be retarding," Gregorios wrote, "but the past is not abandonable. In Western liberalism there is often a misplaced hope of creating a future unrelated to the past. Nehru shared this wrong hope with his fellow liberals in the West. We know now that the past is not dead and that it cannot simply be divested or revoked or broken away from."

The diplomat and former foreign secretary S. K. Singh, talking to a Delhi audience in 1991 about tourism and Indian culture—the speech in which he divided the world neatly into devotees and detractors of India—remarked on India's singular ability to discard nothing civilizational in the course of its development. Every kind of thought and style of living, the diplomat said, is absorbed into "a vast incandescent Indianness" in which all survives. "Even today, in the last decade of the twentieth century, we are carrying our Stone Age with us," he said. "This is neither a negative nor a positive thing. Just a very Indian one."

II

DAILY REALITIES

3

An Image Remade in Violence

INDIA APPROACHES THE TWENTY-FIRST CENTURY hoping that a reformist economic policy and a less ideological, if not idiosyncratic, attitude toward foreign affairs will unleash the considerable untapped potential of this giant nation and secure it a long-sought place among industrial powers. Not a few foreign economists share this hope; they see in India's vast labor pool and growing consumer market a rival to neighboring China, whose economic development, however bold, is prone to political setbacks as an aging leadership tries to hold back a democratic tide. But investment is slow to come to India; obstacles to a free market persist in the bureaucracy and among political parties opposed to the precipitous privatization of nationalized industries and the end of state planning in a country where social and economic gaps yawn wide. Not only socialists have qualms. Indian entrepreneurs and independent social scientists have been cautioning that a free-market economic policy is not enough in a country with a low level of human resource development, a high population growth rate, rapid depletion of natural resources, poor infrastructure, and a high level of violence, much of it politically inspired. Though most of us would still bet on Indian resilience to pull this huge nation through its most challenging years, it seems clear that the political system will have to be purged by the Indian people themselves and a new order of social priorities set for the world's second most populous nation. Some glimpses of daily life, work, and thought in India may serve as an outline of the problems nearly a billion Indians face at home as they try to take their place in the world.

India tumbled into the last decade of the twentieth century tripping unexpectedly over fallen monuments to itself. In one tumultuous year, 1990, three bitter eruptions tore into the country's body and soul, each undermining another of the modern myths around which Indians had been erecting self-congratulatory national images for more than forty years. Mother India would never look quite the same in Indian or foreign eyes.

The year began with the Kashmir Valley in open revolt. The state of Jammu and Kashmir, a Hindu maharaja's kingdom until its incorporation into India under controversial circumstances in 1947, is India's only Muslim-majority state. Although Kashmiri grievances had little or nothing to do with religion, those who took to the streets demanding self-determination shattered the myth that India was one big happy family of differing faiths and cultures living inside immutable frontiers. Kashmiris no longer feel they are part of the Indian union; only the Indian Army keeps them there. India has begun to pay the price of the Nehru dynasty's shortsighted policies in Kashmir, as it has been paying a bloody, tragic price in Punjab since the early 1980s.

In August 1990, caste war broke out in northern India when Prime Minister Vishwanath Pratap Singh, who had been promising for more than a year (as a candidate and then as a newly elected head of government) to put into practice a dormant, decade-old affirmative action program for perennially disadvantaged lower-caste Indians, did exactly what he said he would do. He prepared to set aside 27 percent of government jobs for the "backward castes," who rank just above casteless untouchables. Twenty-two and a half percent of these federal jobs were already reserved for outcastes and tribal people. Stunned by the audacity of this political visionary with princely lineage, the country's outraged higher-caste youth objected violently to his attack on their privilege, egged on by Singh's opportunistic political opponents. More than two hundred upper-caste young men and women, some only boys and girls, set fire to themselves, or were set ablaze by hysterical cohorts; twelve died, according to a report by the People's Union for Democratic Rights, an Indian group that attempted to conduct a dispassionate investigation of the phenomenon.

A month later, a huge demonstration in New Delhi, swarming with gangs of toughs armed with iron rods and rocks (the worst of the lot loyal to Prime Minister Singh's recently dismissed deputy prime minister, Devi Lal, the erstwhile political boss of Haryana state) brought a new level of ugly brute behavior to protests in a country where violent demonstrations are commonplace. At the same time, and not entirely coincidentally, new parties of outcaste and lower-caste Indians were drawing huge crowds to rallies where speaker after speaker denounced as hypocrisy the Indian establishment's professed belief in egalitarianism. This, ironically, was the year set aside to honor the 100th birth anniversary of Ambedkar, the untouchable constitutionalist who died at odds with Hinduism and the ruling Congress Party over the unending scourge of caste discrimination. More than three decades after his death, it seemed that almost nothing had changed. Constitutional guarantees of equality began sounding more hollow.

And then, in October 1990, a horde of frenzied Hindu zealots forced their way into the grounds of the Babri Masjid, the heavily guarded, disputed mosque in the holy city of Ayodhya, where they vandalized what they could and then hoisted over its weary domes the saffron flags of Hinduism, a prelude to the December 1992 mob demolition of the sixteenth-century building and the start of construction on a temple to the mythological Lord Rama. On the streets and highways of Uttar Pradesh, screaming, hyperventilating mobs stopped cars and forced their occupants to join in shouting "Jai Sri Ram!" The phrase, meaning "Hail Lord Rama," was also the greeting of the day in state government offices in Lucknow, and it was spoken with a frightening depth and intensity, recalling the "Bande Mataram!" or roughly "Hail to the Motherland" of the pre-independence Bengali nationalist movement. *The Pioneer*, a distinguished North Indian newspaper, trumpeted on its front page the opinion that the fevered desecration of the little mosque was a glorious event to be remembered for a thousand years. A third image, that of a secular India, was cracking.

A few weeks after the 1990 storming of the Babri Masjid, Prime Minister Singh was out of office, having lost the support of the Hindu revivalist Bharatiya Janata Party (several of whose leaders had been arrested on their way to Ayodhya). He had already alienated the upper castes and much of the middle class on the issue of affirmative action. Industrialists joined his foes. Raymonds, one of India's largest textile companies, temporarily converted advertising billboards to giant posters depicting rising flames and carrying the simple message: "Today, this space is reserved for India's martyrs." The word "reserved" was painted in red, a slap at the "reservation" of jobs for the disadvantaged castes. No one had suggested that affirmative action would be forced on the private sector. India is a long way from that. In late 1992, two years after the fall of his government, V. P. Singh's policy was upheld in principle if not in detail by the Supreme Court of India. But by then the Singh administration was history.

In the end, the political left alone stood by Singh in 1990 as disloyal politicians in his own centrist Janata Dal organization and governing National Front coalition delivered the final blows not only to his government but also to the hope of a genuine, secular, two-party system finally developing in India. Principles—political ethics, the need to alleviate the plight of the oppressed, the commitment to protect religious minorities—never entered the argument. The opportunists had found a quick way to settle scores and grab power, a few enriching themselves along the way by selling their loyalty to Singh's enemies. Millions of rupees changed hands.

It was not only the unity of India, its constitutional guarantees against caste discrimination, and its cloak of secularism that were torn asunder in 1990. The three crises exposed enormous lapses in the professed objectivity of the press and other media, including the best of the private news videos, *Newstrack,* which slid into irrational invective against Prime Minister Singh. The media are dominated by upper-caste Hindus who know how small a minority they are—scarcely 10 percent of the population. Their instinctive response was not unlike that of white South Africans who find the idea of majority rule too terrible to contemplate. The liberalism of the intellectual elite was severely tested and often found wanting.

Ashis Nandy, an eminent political scientist, does not count himself among the admirers of the report prepared in 1980 by the Bihari politician Bindeshwari Pathak Mandal, on which Prime Minister Singh based his affirmative action plan. "I doubt if the Indian state can bring about the kind of social changes the report presumes," he wrote at the height of the crisis. But he added that "the anti-Mandal stir has revealed an aspect of the Indian elite—including many of my friends and colleagues—which I wish I had not seen." N. Ram, a crusading southern journalist who edits *Frontline* magazine in Madras, thought that the press had sunk to its lowest ebb since independence in reporting on the Mandal disturbances. In conversations, Ram, a Brahmin, a graduate of Columbia University's Graduate School of Journalism, and a former correspondent in the United States for *The Hindu* newspaper, compared the attitude of the Indian upper castes with the racism of the pre–civil rights days in the American South.

The year of turmoil fanned old resentments in South India, where caste and religious fanaticism are largely yesterday's issues and Kashmir and Punjab seem a world away. There were no large demonstrations against the Mandal report in southern cities—or in Bombay, the hub of private capital, where government jobs are not so highly prized. In the South, where affirmative action plans for the lower castes, some a century old, are so well established that Brahmins are organizing to project themselves as an endangered species, the nation's most progressive people were forced to watch northerners pulling each other apart, paralyzing the all-powerful central government. Southerners have long bristled at the domination of a northern Hindi-speaking culture, which led to language riots in what is now Tamil Nadu in the early years of independence and, ultimately, the creation of linguistically defined states in the South. The irritation is growing again, in a new generation. At Bangalore and Madras universities and other southern institutions, students say Hindi chauvinism is being forced down their throats by the national television network, Doordarshan. The recent serializations of Hindu Indian classics are widely regarded as "northern" versions of the epics. The choice in 1991 of a southern-born prime minister, P. V. Narasimha Rao, did not mitigate the alienation.

"Delhi is fast losing its image as a responsive capital of a multipolar, multilingual country," says V. K. Madhavan Kutty, one of the South's best-known journalists, who insists that he feels like "an alien without a visa" in the Indian capital. He calls the dominant politicians of the North "feudal chieftains defending a culture we in the South had demolished long ago." To cosmopolitan southerners, North India seems a cold, rough, introverted place, insensitive to cultural nuances. As more documents begin to emanate from New Delhi written in Hindi only, southerners are beginning to feel colonized. "The North will not be able to rule us with a mere language," Madhavan Kutty once wrote. "We know only the language of culture, tradition and decency, and that alone will contribute to what is called Indian unity. We want to tell the North that they should listen to these yet-gentle voices before they turn into the shrill note of alienation and tragedy, before it all degenerates into a conflict between the colonies and the colonizers."

At the end of January 1991, a few months after the defeat of the V. P. Singh administration, a large southern state became the latest victim of Delhi politics, an example of what rankles voters far from the capital. The popularly elected state government of Tamil Nadu, which was led by a political ally of Singh, was summarily thrown out of office by Prime Minister Chandra Shekhar, apparently at the behest of Rajiv Gandhi, who was hoping to win back the state for the Congress Party. The state's chief minister, Muthuvel Karunanidhi, and his Tamil nationalist party, the Dravidian Munnetra Kazhagam, were accused of allowing law and order to break down and permitting Sri Lankan Tamil guerrillas to operate freely there. The charges, which stretched the Indian constitution's intended definition of an emergency situation, were both incredible and ironic. Tamil Nadu was among the most peaceful of Indian states when its government was evicted and replaced with rule from New Delhi through the appointed governor—who, incidentally, was also replaced; the incumbent, Surjit Singh Barnala, could not condone the charade. Everyone knew that Indira Gandhi and Karunanidhi's late rival, the film star–politician M. G. Ramachandran, had been the first and most important sponsors of the Sri Lankan militants in the state. In power in Madras, Karunanidhi was only following their lead.

Three months after the dismissal of the Karunanidhi government, when Tamil Nadu was in hands friendlier to Congress and presumably safer under central government rule, Rajiv Gandhi was murdered there, apparently by these same Sri Lankan Tamil nationalists. No one dismissed the new governor for failing to police the state. Sadly for Indian democracy, Karunanidhi was never able to make his widely criticized ouster a successful issue in the state election that followed in June, an indicator of slipping respect for institutions and democratic procedures among the electorate, who, tired of the Karunanidhi government at midterm, simply fell in line behind the Congress Party policy of Realpolitik and took a gamble on his rivals. No judge was willing to step in and restore a constitutionally elected government. A Congress ally and leader of the late Ramachandran's party, Jayalalitha Jayaram, who had also been the screen idol's co-star and companion, became the new chief minister of Tamil Nadu, and proceeded to institute a regime far more autocratic than that of her predecessor.

When I asked Gandhi in the last interview before his assassination about North-South differences (we were near Madras) and other more violent regional problems, he could only reiterate his intense commitment to strong central government and restate his evident fears of more secessionist movements in India. He never seemed to appreciate the need for ameliorating concessions to regional autonomy as a tactic against further disaffection. While acknowledging, for example, that regional broadcasting centers would have to be given some freedom to promote local languages and cultures, a demand of southern Indians and a potential safety valve anywhere, he insisted that "they should not be allowed to end up as regional chauvinisms." The longer India delays a reform of broadcasting and allows Hindi speakers of the North to dominate television and radio, however, the more those regional chauvinisms will grow of their own accord. Madhavan Kutty calls Doordarshan, the national television network, "the worst enemy of integration."

The legacy of four decades of Congress Party, Nehru-Gandhi family government has begun to haunt and torment India, making victims of its own leaders. Prime Minister Indira Gandhi, whose administrations in 1965–1977 and 1980–1984 left democratic institutions substantially weakened, demonstrated during the Emergency of 1975–1977, when civil liberties were suspended and journalists jailed, that her political survival was more important than the system. She meddled in Punjab, trying to weaken Sikh leadership by encouraging splits. In a cynical move, she propped up the Sikh fanatic Jarnail Singh Bhindranwale until his armed movement got out of her control. She then sent the Indian Army into the Sikhs' holiest shrine, the Golden Temple in Amritsar, to defeat the radicals. Tanks crashed down the marble steps to the interior courtyard with its sacred "tank" or pool, killing pilgrims at prayer along with Bhindranwale and his gang. Holy buildings were shelled and an archive destroyed. Bodies were hauled away in garbage trucks.

In October 1984, Indira Gandhi fell victim to the deadly backlash against her partisan tampering, just as her son and successor also became a victim seven years later of policies gone tragically wrong when he died at the hands of foreign assassins who had once been the beneficiaries of her shortsighted attempt to destabilize the small, rapidly developing neighboring nation of Sri Lanka, too pro-Western to coexist with her viscerally anti-American phobias. Indira Gandhi and her son Rajiv lived long enough to sow the seeds of another rebellion, in Kashmir, where in 1983–1984 she undercut and split the National Conference party of Farooq Abdullah, son of Sheikh Abdullah, a popular nationalist known as the Lion of Kashmir. Farooq Abdullah's crime was refusing to share power in Jammu and Kashmir with the Congress Party. Four years later, Farooq Abdullah would be forced into an electoral alliance with Rajiv Gandhi in a state poll so corrupted by vote-rigging and other irregularities that it completed the alienation of a generation of young Muslim Kashmiris already venting other grievances: the underdevelopment of their region, the squandering of revenues by corrupt officials, poor transportation links to the rest of India, a refusal to allow Srinagar's airport to open to international traffic to boost tourism, and the domination of the state administration and public services in the Kashmir Valley by Hindus—the Kashmiri Pandits, Nehru's ancestral community. The National Front's alliance with Congress, an "Indian" party, left nowhere for Kashmiri nationalists to go but to the armed independence movement—and to Pakistan for guns.

Through years of civil strife under several governments, Indian leaders failed to recognize (or learn from their erstwhile Soviet friends) that force alone, with or without gestures of reconciliation, cannot hold the nation together. Increasingly, the Indian Army and paramilitaries of the Central Reserve Police Force, the Border Security Force, or the Indo-Tibetan Border Patrol were brought in to confront or quell civil disruptions that cried for creative and conciliatory political solutions. Large areas of the country fell under effective martial law; in 1990, soldiers and police were given the right to shoot on sight in Kashmir with no regard to due process. Troops and police already employed such powers recklessly in Punjab. The army, bruised and demoralized by an ill-fated adventure in Sri Lanka from 1987 to 1990, became more and more undisciplined, particularly in Punjab, Kashmir, and the northeastern state of Assam, where abuses of human rights are now as cruel as they are commonplace. Lives are taken, property destroyed, women and children abused. Day by day, year by year, thousands more Indians taste alienation, or turn to violence themselves.

In a prescient speech made in 1987, Myron Weiner, a political scientist at the Massachusetts Institute of Technology who, unlike many Westerners, has been consistently clear-headed and unromantic in his writings on India, suggested that managing crises among India's nationalities could be a major problem for New Delhi through the rest of the century.

"That India has done so well with its political institutions over the past forty years is a cause for some optimism," he told an audience of international scholars meeting in Jerusalem. "Commitment to the maintenance of a single country and to a democratic process is strong where it counts—among the national elite, the military and the bureaucracy, the professional classes, the business community, the national politicians. However, faced with the choice of exercising coercive authority to maintain a single country or remaining democratic, most of the elite would choose the former over the latter. If need be, the center would exercise all the force at its command to prevent secession, even if it meant a suspension of democratic rights." By 1990 this had happened.

In the last decade of the twentieth century, India's increasingly transparent failures to honor and protect its people's civil and humanitarian rights incurred the opprobrium of a lengthening list of international human rights organizations and several foreign government watchdog bodies, including committees of the British Parliament and American Congress. The United States Department of State noted in its annual human rights report for India that by 1990, political killing by security forces was taking place in Kashmir "on an increasingly wide scale."

The problem is not confined to Kashmir. Figures compiled independently show that across the nation more Indians are the victims of their own army or police each year than, for example, the total number of Chileans who died during the seventeen-year dictatorship of Agosto Pinochet. A Chilean presidential commission reported in 1991 that about two thousand people had been tortured to death by Pinochet's police. Nearly a thousand more than that died in only three days in New Delhi in the November 1984 politically inspired massacre of Sikhs that followed Mrs. Gandhi's assassination by Sikh bodyguards. When paramilitary police fired on an unarmed funeral procession in Srinagar on May 21, 1990, dozens of people were killed in a few moments of panic. The incident was comparable to the attack eighteen months later on mourners at a cemetery in the disputed territory East Timor by the Indonesian Army, an outrage that brought down on Jakarta the worldwide condemnation New Delhi had escaped. Thousands continue to die annually in Punjab, Assam, and Kashmir, some killed by militants but many others shot in faked gun battles or other encounters with security forces or in house-to-house searches. They are described on the evening news as "unidentified terrorists." Ranjit Singh Narula, retired chief justice of the Punjab and Haryana High Courts, drew this to my attention. "Think about it," he said, "*Unidentified* terrorists."

No other large country has enjoyed India's inexplicable immunity to censure and sanction. A nation wrapped for half a century in the aura of the Mahatma Gandhi and the glamor of the Raj was always able to demonstrate its essentially democratic nature. Those days are fast disappearing as democratic governments take hold throughout South Asia and a less glamorous India is being discovered. In 1990 and 1991, Amnesty International began publishing sweeping surveys of the generally deteriorating situation throughout the country. Among its findings: legal safeguards against human rights violations fall short of international standards, thousands of Indians are being held without charge or trial, torture and abuse of prisoners is widespread, and more than fifty people a year die in police custody, disappearances and extrajudicial executions are on the rise, and the right of habeas corpus is difficult for the poor to obtain. Amnesty International also noted that the armed forces have powers in disturbed areas that all but obliterate basic civil liberties in the world's most populous democracy, and that military excesses can be shielded from investigation merely by the invocation of national security.

Official India's repeated protestations of its commitment to democracy and due process are taking on the ring of meaningless mantras. Myron Weiner, in a 1991 book on *The Child and the State in India*, called much of Indian social legislation involving untouchability, child labor, child marriage, or the dowry system "statements of intentions" rather than functioning laws. "The words used in the legislation are a kind of modern talisman intended to bring results by the magical power of the words themselves," he wrote. Legislation, he observed, was meant to show that Indian governments were "committed to all that is modern and progressive." If laws are not enforced the fault lies with society, those in power say. In areas of unrest, separatists and militants are blamed for the climate of fear.

4

Whose India?

W HAT KIND OF COUNTRY IS THIS, where the murder of yet another young wife by her in-laws may get equal space in the press with the marriage of a neem tree to a peepul tree? Where scientists launch missiles and the head of a university journalism department tells me in complete seriousness that American spy satellites cut out over the ashram of the guru Sai Baba, so great is his mental power? Where tens of thousands of uncontrolled industries pollute a river and a gaggle of swamis pour thousands of gallons of milk in it to cleanse it? "Is there no law in this country, where millions of people are dying without a morsel of food, to prosecute senseless cranks?" a letter writer named S. Balachandra asked a newspaper. At least it's a country that still fights back.

Indians like to think that they inhabit the most diverse nation on earth, and many take a certain pride in John Kenneth Galbraith's description of their system as a "functioning anarchy." While the claim to a unique anthropological or even cultural diversity would not survive a visit to New York, Los Angeles, or Jakarta, there are many Indias, separated from each other not only by language, religion, ethnicity, or geography, but also by historical time. Pockets of medieval life (or S. K. Singh's Stone Age) survive in a country with microwave kitchens. There is also the pervasive, resilient apartheid of caste in all its obvious and subtle manifestations. Some social scientists, for example, suggest that a good deal of the knee-jerk hostility among the intellectual elite to private entrepreneurial success is rooted in the Brahmin's contempt for the Bania, the subcaste of business and commerce, and the caste of Mahatma Gandhi.

In a country where rigorous public analysis of politics and society is confined to a handful of think tanks and a few newspaper and magazine columnists—and Parliament has all but ceased to debate substantive issues—there is a new awareness from the grassroots up that India is less sure of itself as it approaches the twenty-first century than it was at independence in 1947. In the back of many Indian minds are troubling questions. Will politicians be tempted to suspend civil liberties again as Indira Gandhi did for far less cause during the Emergency? Will the military move too close to the center of power? Will parties that are increasingly described as fascist in organization gain ground as mobs become the only outlet for mushrooming jobless populations and the underemployed underclasses?

Many Indians still find reasons to be hopeful, believing that a democratic system of some kind fits into their tradition, contrary to the evidence of much of their history. K. Natwar Singh, the Congress Party politician and former minister of state for foreign affairs—he who was doleful in his view of a Hindu's relationship with facts, writing on one occasion that "our cerebral underpinning rests on a sponge"—insists that uncertainty and unrest are part of the process of the evolution of Indian democracy, and that something more durable must emerge from the turmoil.

"The strength of this country lies in the decent, honest hardworking people who do their jobs," he said over coffee in his elegant parlor as another election campaign was about to begin. "These people make this country work. That this secular, democratic Indian experiment works is one of the great political miracles of the twentieth century. There are areas of moral backsliding. There is corruption, there is skullduggery, and there is greed, but the country works. This congested, complicated, large country runs. There is an innate wisdom and sagacity that makes the right decisions—and this in a society which was until very recently an oral society."

"But," said Natwar Singh—a soft-spoken intellectual whose book-filled home has the atmosphere of a sophisticated salon, in sharp contrast to the usual graceless, smudgy, rough-and-tumble abode of an Indian politician— "it is true that this is a society in the process of turmoil, change. Secularism is being attacked. There is no way this country can survive without secularism. On caste, the dialectics of what V. P. Singh has let loose will take a long time to work out, but work out they have to. The major political parties in India, including the Congress, have been losing their traditional supporters, who feel that these parties are dominated by the upper-caste elite."

Natwar Singh, born into a princely family in Rajasthan in the days of maharajas, digressed for a moment to tell the story of the time in 1984 when he made up his mind to leave the foreign service to plunge into electoral politics, and went to Indira Gandhi to announce his decision. Always exquisitely dressed, he joked that he would now have to acquire a new wardrobe for the hustings, where rumpled white cotton is de rigueur for high-born men trying to demonstrate their oneness with the masses. The imperious prime minister looked him over for a few seconds and retorted: "Now that you're coming into politics, a thicker skin would be more useful."

"At any given point in all this turmoil and churning, 98 percent of India is peaceful," said Natwar Singh, resuming his analysis. "But how unrealistic can we be? No political party in its manifesto lays any stress on family planning. It's considered political dynamite, electoral dynamite. But some day, all Indian parties are going to have to sit down and say that this is a national issue. Before we can even dream of making life more comfortable for the few, we must make it bearable for the many. Two hundred million of our people live in reasonable comfort. Another two hundred million live in uncomfortable comfort. The rest have a pretty thin time."

"And the census!" he said of the 1991 count of Indians, which revealed a growth rate still over 2 percent and great disparities in quality of life among Indians. "Can you imagine the meager coverage given by the press to the census figures? It should have been the most important story in every paper every day for one week. The pressure of numbers is colossal. How do you build schools for 16 or 17 million people every year?"

"In Nehru's letters to state chief ministers, from 1947 to 1951, there was no mention of family planning," recalled Natwar Singh, a scholar and defender of India's founding generation of leaders, who are now under attack for failing to put more emphasis on population control and the development of human resources. "But India was underpopulated then. No one anticipated the health revolution, the revolution of antibiotics. From 1851 to 1931 our population remained pretty much the same. As for Gandhiji's celibacy and self-control route to family planning—he could do it, but it was expecting too much of others."

Natwar Singh is among that cosmopolitan minority more often pained than flattered by persistent praise from Westerners enthralled by the Indian's inattention to detail, ability to lead an unexamined life, rejection of reality, resignation to fate, escape into the otherworldly when the world around is closing in. Writing in *Sunday* magazine in March 1991, when the country was in political flux, he said this about the British poet Katherine Raine's contribution to the Western romantic genre, a book called *India Seen Afar:* "I finished reading this book with mixed feelings. Admiration on the one hand, despair on the other," he wrote, before zeroing in on Raine's paean to the "blessed gift of inattention." "Alas!" he says. "We as a people and a nation have paid a heavy price for inattention."

In one of the most significant (and underpublicized) surveys of day-to-day life around the world, the United Nations Development Program in 1991 ranked India 123rd among 160 Third World nations on a Human Development Index measured by longevity, access to knowledge, and reasonably decent living standards. For quality of life, India trailed behind all of Latin America (except Haiti), most of Asia (except the immediate neighborhood), and some Sub-Saharan African nations. In India, the report found,

370 million people had no access to clean water and more than 400 million lived below a locally computed poverty line, usually measured by the income necessary to maintain a minimal caloric intake. About 30 percent of babies were born with low birth weights (compared with 12 percent in Thailand or 17 percent in Ghana). India spent less than one percent of its gross national product on health care (compared with 2.4 percent in Brazil or 2.8 percent in Jamaica). Indians own about 78 radios and 7 television sets per 1,000 people (an important gauge of availability of information). In neighboring Sri Lanka, there are 191 radios and 31 television sets per 1,000; in Mexico, the comparative figures are 241 radios and 120 television receivers. India, which calls itself a socialist republic, has no social security system or comprehensive national health service. Small district hospitals function in intense heat without air-conditioned operating theaters or intensive care units. In the winter, I saw nurses in a North Indian teaching hospital huddled in overcoats in unheated wards where leaves blew around beds with soiled sheets and torn blankets.

5

Mother India's Children

R.K. NARAYAN, the storyteller whose evocative yarns spun around the imaginary town of Malgudi have brought a glimpse of South Indian village life and its quirks to a world of readers, sat on the nondescript sofa in his nondescript government-assigned apartment in New Delhi and talked about his first speech in the Rajya Sabha, the upper house of the Indian Parliament, to which he had been appointed by the government in recognition of his distinguished international literary career. The apartment came with the honor. Members of both houses of the Indian Parliament get free housing in New Delhi, a perk of office that allows those who already live in the capital to rent their own property for a profit and cling like barnacles to the government-issue house or flat for weeks and months after an election defeat. Narayan, on the other hand, lived in Madras and rarely came to the capital, where the atmosphere never inspired him. He was indifferent to the little flat. In his eighties when we first met, he wanted to talk about children, the subject of his speech to the Rajya Sabha.

His address had caused a minor sensation. First-timers' speeches were expected to be long-winded, self-serving puffery on ponderous subjects. Narayan talked about school bags, crowded classes, and learning regimes that stifled the innate creativity of the young. Applause came from parents all over India.

"I did this deliberately," he said, always impish and enjoying a good joke played on the establishment, ever since his boyhood days. "I was never serious. The trouble is, I'm still not serious. This kind of attitude can make you a writer, or a bum." His concern for the young, however, was real.

"Politics and political life take up too much of our attention," he said, explaining why he, at eighty-three, had decided to speak for the nation's officially voiceless little girls and boys. "There are important basic things to be done that we are not doing. These politicians are concerned with such dreadfully serious problems. But the whole adult world is ignoring children. Not only poor children, but also rich children are suffering. Children in general have to be protected more from adults. Children should not be forced to work so hard. They should not be taken out to walk in political processions and carry banners in demonstrations."

Narayan, a keen observer of detail, had been noticing how contemporary India's children were trudging to school slumped forward with pounds of textbooks in backpack-style schoolbags. In most overcrowded and under-equipped government schools and a majority of the intensely competitive private schools, there are no assigned desks or lockers, and pupils often carry with them everything they might possibly need in the course of a school day. To be caught without the right book can bring punishment in a rigid system that still owes a lot to Victorian England.

"You know, sometimes children have to go a long distance to reach a school, walking," Narayan said. "But even when they climb on a van or a bus, what happens when they step up? The weight pulls them back. I've always been an enemy of schoolbags. And schools, also. Children must not be bothered so much. They must be left to grow by themselves, and some other system of education must be thought of that doesn't involve so much learning by rote."

"Our schools give too much homework," Narayan went on. "A child comes home and works all evening and goes to bed. He gets up in the morning and goes back to school. They have no time for play. If they were left alone, they could at least have time to look at trees and birds, and run about in the streets and play among themselves. They don't have time for that. This system of education is crushing them."

Narayan was talking about the education of the more privileged children, which almost always means those plodding off in starched uniforms to private schools. It would be hard to find a middle class family willing to have a child educated in a neighborhood government school in India. The fear that a toddler will not find a place in a good private institution breeds an anxiety that would not be unfamiliar to Manhattan families. But in India, where there are many more people and far fewer places, the anguish is multiplied many times. The most sought after education is in Christian, often Roman Catholic, institutions found in all major Indian cities and in mountain towns where boarding schools were set up by missionaries in colonial times. So popular are the generically labeled "convent" schools in Hindu India that private establishments in no way linked to churches, and certainly not staffed by nuns, tack "convent" onto their names in the hope of attracting clients.

Nationalistic Hindus who rail against Western culture are not averse to begging for a place in a Catholic school for a son or daughter, who can expect to get a superior education in a disciplined environment, a prerequisite to university entrance or a good job. A dozen years or more of slogging through a no-nonsense convent school does bring results. Young Indians do brilliant work in higher education abroad, particularly in the United States, where tens of thousands now study at the undergraduate or graduate level.

Even professional anti-Americans, who expend a good deal of energy trashing the materialism of American life, seem to see nothing hypocritical in opting for universities and colleges in the United States, where students can reliably expect an uninterrupted education. The politicization of Indian universities often paralyzes teaching, as faculty factions square off over curriculum or personnel choices. Campuses have branches or "youth wings" of national parties, which fight student elections (sometimes violently) on issues that have little to do with campus life. Strikes are common and universities are closed at the first sign of unrest. Academic decisions are made for political reasons and appointments or promotions are sometimes held up for months or even years because of partisan squabbling or the unwillingness of administrators to buck a rigid seniority system. The psychoanalyst Sudhir Kakar, writing more generally on Indian society, says that "the hierarchical principle of social organization has been central to the conservation of Indian tradition, but it can only be a source of stagnation in modern institutions whose purpose is scientific inquiry or technological development."

Teaching salaries are low in higher education. A political scientist at Jawaharlal Nehru University in New Delhi, holding down one of India's most sought-after academic jobs, said that on a salary of a few hundred dollars a month he could not afford to subscribe to the basic journals in his field or buy the books he would like to own. Equipment is minimal or nonexistent. When I arrived at Punjab University's department of journalism in 1980 as a visiting professor, it was a surprise to find lecture halls devoid of typewriters or any other tools of the trade. Journalism, the most hands-on of subjects, was being taught more or less by dictation, with no scope for practical training. Students looked askance at suggestions that they spend their own time on mock reporting assignments. And this was the best and oldest journalism school on the Subcontinent.

Convent schools and campus politics are, however, pretty much the preserve of a small Indian elite. Most Indians don't go to school at all, or get only intermittent formal education in early childhood. The extravagances of India's fast-developing urban plutocracy, including private and foreign education, are centuries removed from the hardscrabble existence of village life, where a majority of Indian children are still born and live. More than a fifth of them will be condemned at birth to untouchability or tribal status, and will encounter universal discrimination and deprivation, however subtly caste distinctions may be enforced. Another 40 percent of Indians are con-

sidered "backward," members of those lower castes with little access to any
of the levers of power. Muslims, at least 11 percent of the population, are
also frequently poor and disadvantaged. India, the heir to great civilizations,
now produces most of the world's illiterates and child laborers. Statistically,
few Indians are born with the hope of enjoying a childhood as other children know it. India and its neighbors Pakistan and Bangladesh account for
one-third of all the children in the world not in school, 45 percent of the
world's undernourished youngsters, and half of all children living in absolute poverty. Forty-one percent of Indian children under the age of five are
underweight, according to figures compiled by the United Nations Development Program.

"In the last decade of the twentieth century, why are we still talking
about child survival?" asked Ashis Bose, an economist and demographer at
Delhi University. "We have some of the best economists in the world, but
one of our major failures has been in communication. We don't know how to
communicate with illiterate people, and this has been a major flaw in all our
programs." He said thirty years of fieldwork had convinced him that warnings about the national population crossing the billion mark means nothing
to the man or woman in the small village that all but circumscribes their
world. The social scientist Rajni Kothari, asked why there was no panic in
government about the future of the great human underbelly of India, the
majority of poor or struggling people, replied that a cynical establishment
hell-bent on burnishing India's technological, middle-class image were prepared to leave a large part of India out of its planning. "Only those who can
enter this bright utopian future are welcome," he said. "The poor are an
embarrassment."

That unseen majority, much of it in the illiterate, impoverished North
where the population is growing faster than the rest of India, is steadily
enlarging the pool of unemployed youth whom politicians use to create slum
"vote banks," intimidate rivals, or swell crowds. The youthful mobs are
becoming ominously larger, more ubiquitous, and more unruly. The thousands of boys and young men trucked into Delhi by the Congress Party to
march in Rajiv Gandhi's funeral procession in May 1991 turned the somber
cremation site into a travesty of grief, jumping on the pyre platform to wave
at television cameras and causing dignitaries and friends of the Gandhi family to scatter.

Myron Weiner's book *The Child and the State in India* attracted an unusual
amount of Indian attention when it appeared early in 1991 because it dared
to speak a hard truth: that India, almost alone among modern nations, has
not made it a priority to take children off the streets and out of an exploited
child labor force to put them in schools. Weiner is among a growing number
of observers who reject the oft-repeated explanation that India is too poor
for universal education, and that disadvantaged families need all available
hands to bring in income. Coupled with excuses for why family planning is

also not a high priority, this indifference toward mass education has led to a situation where fewer than half of India's children between the ages of six and fourteen are in school, despite Indian claims that there is universal primary education. Most Indians, including educators themselves, don't consider this a serious enough problem to make it a political or even an educational issue. A scholar in Delhi found that his child's modern history textbook contained thirty-two pages on Nehru, eighteen on the 1918 Russian Revolution, and none on India's development problems.

"India's low per capita income and economic situation is less relevant as an explanation than the belief systems of the state bureaucracy, a set of beliefs that are widely shared by educators, social activists, trade unionists, academic researchers and, more broadly, by members of the Indian middle class," Weiner concluded. "At the core of these beliefs are the Indian view of the social order, notions concerning the upper and lower strata, the role of education as a means of maintaining differentiations among social classes and concerns that 'excessive' and 'inappropriate' education for the poor would disrupt existing social arrangements." In other words, illiteracy insures that the masses will remain powerless.

A century earlier, the Hindu reformer Vivekananda made the same, now largely forgotten, points. Amiya Kumar Mazumdar, a follower of the Swami, wrote in a small book called *Understanding Vivekananda* that the reformer came back from travels in the West convinced that "education, education and education alone" was the only way to uplift the poor. Mazumdar quoted Vivekananda thus: "Traveling through the many cities of Europe and observing in them the comforts and education of even the poor people, there was brought to my mind the state of our own poor people, and I used to shed tears. What made the difference? Education was the answer I got." One hundred years later, the task of educating the poor has been made much more difficult through decades of neglect. It is doubtful that India will in the foreseeable future have the resources to introduce mass compulsory education, even if there were a political will to do so.

With the flow of information through village India limited by illiteracy and poor communications systems, many Indian mothers rely on local medical practitioners for advice on family planning as well as treatment for themselves and their children. Practitioners of India's three indigenous medical systems—ayurvedic, homeopathic, and unani; all holistic in approach, keeping the body "in balance," with or without the use of natural or synthetic drugs—are often very effective in dealing with common illnesses. But they are apparently much less useful in family planning and child health, according to a 1988 survey made for the Ministry of Health and Family Welfare by the Center for Research, Planning and Action, a private organization in New Delhi. The survey, titled *A Study of Knowledge, Attitude and Practice of ISM* [Indian Systems of Medicine] *Practitioners in the Context of Delivery of Family Welfare Services,* discovered that more than half of homeopathic and unani doctors and 39.5 percent of better-educated ayurvedic practitioners thought that girls should marry before the legal age of eighteen, which may help to explain why the law is largely ignored in many rural areas. These doctors, the survey said, "are not serious about controlling the growth of population by recommending late marriage for girls." Between 41 and 62 percent of the traditional doctors questioned said that a woman who stopped taking an oral contraceptive could not become pregnant for at least fifteen days; a smaller percentage replied that the safe period went on for two or three months. Between a quarter and 55 percent of doctors, whether or not they replied to the question, admitted that they did not really know much about oral contraceptives. More than 90 percent of practitioners surveyed had no training in family planning and few had any knowledge of childhood immunization or oral rehydration therapy.

In Rajasthan, where the population growth rate is one of the highest in India, women told me that they would have fewer children if there were safe medical clinics and doctors they could trust not to make them ill through contaminated equipment used for sterilization—still the most common form of birth control in many parts of India—or unsafe intrauterine devices or contraceptives. "What will happen to my children if I get sick or die?" is a common response to questions about why family planning had not been considered. Responsibility for contraception inevitably falls on the Indian woman, who then runs the added risk of being punished by her husband for seeking family planning help.

"The people know there is no room in the house, no space on the bus," said Dr. Devendra Kothari, at the Institute of Health Management Research in Jaipur, the Rajasthani state capital. In Rajasthan, girls are frequently married off by their families when they are as young as ten or twelve, though these marriages may not be consummated until after puberty. Kothari says that because comparatively few children are born out of wedlock in India, enforcing the legal marriage age of eighteen for girls would make a significant difference, a point made by most demographers. Enforcement would require a major attitudinal change on two counts: girls would have to be given the freedom and encouragement to make something other than wives of themselves, and communities would have to be willing to report parents who force underage daughters into marriage. Kothari is more optimistic than most experts that social attitudes could be altered if more effort and ingenuity went into the cause of family planning.

"Everyone feels the growing population," he said. "Even men don't want so many babies. They have to find the money to feed them." Kothari debunks the standard excuses why Rajasthanis continue to have six or more children. His extensive research in the state found that there is no dearth of information on family planning, and that low female literacy rates (as miserable as 2 or 3 percent in some areas) do not mean that women cannot understand the concepts and consequences of contraception. "Don't confuse literacy with rationality," he said. "The people who built the Taj Mahal didn't have Harvard degrees."

And the desire for more sons? The Hindu precept that a son should light his parents' funeral pyres is often given as a reason for producing more children than families need or want in order to insure a surviving male offspring. "Every Indian now wants two sons and a daughter," said Kothari, who argues that many people would prefer to stop at that number. Kothari says that village people are aware that their children have a better chance of survival with access to immunization and are less concerned than officials think they are about childhood deaths. "Infant mortality is a scapegoat," he said. "In Rajasthan, 28 percent of the pregnancies are unwanted and many are ending in abortions, a form of birth control. Many people are going to private abortion clinics. You can see them advertised on trains." Kothari's extensive research in Rajasthan confirms what village women say: that they don't need any more propaganda about family planning, they just need better services. They shy away from government-run "sterilization camps," filthy temporary centers where women are forced to sit or lie on the ground, are subjected to assembly-line operations and treated as statistics, numbers to help meet the national target. Behind the "successful" statistics, however, are often different realities. Mothers are often sterilized after having half a dozen or more children, when they consider their normal reproductive life nearly over. If most of those children live, this hardly amounts to population control.

At Delhi University's Institute of Economic Growth, Ashis Bose said he heard an award-winning doctor boast that he could do 600 laparoscopies in one day. "He should have been arrested, not rewarded," Bose said. He believes that the concept of targets and the fascination with the technology of family planning were introduced by Western, especially American, family planning experts, along with the idea of cash incentives. "Looking back, the three American ideas—high technology, the lure of money, and the use of a bureaucracy with targets to meet—all have failed."

In Jaipur, Kothari said that the first step toward a successful population control program in India would be to take family planning out of the Ministry of Health, a huge department far removed from village life. Family planning is not, incidentally, called family planning in India. That terminology has been out of favor since the mid 1970s when Sanjay Gandhi, Indira Gandhi's political heir until his death in a stunt plane in 1980, was using coercive techniques to force men to undergo vasectomies. India officially calls the service "family welfare" and treats it as part of medical care. Kothari argues that women who seek help with contraception or sterilization are not ill and should be treated as VIPs in cheerful, purpose-built family planning clinics staffed by specialists. Like Bose, with whom he does not always agree about means and ends, Kothari also argues that the system of giving cash incentives or a gift (in one Rajasthani area it was beads) should be abolished. A small insurance policy against future medical care would be a far better reward. "Why bribe poor people with 200 rupees for a sterilization?" he asks. "This sends the wrong message. By having a small family, they will improve their lives and their incomes—it will be its own reward. Put the 200 rupees into insurance against death or disability or side effects of a sterilization."

It is inconceivable that India will not pay a heavy price for its neglect of its poor women and children, the creators of tomorrow's nation. It is often argued that there is already too much education, too many unemployed university graduates, and far too many applicants for almost any job, whatever the qualifications required. But that view may be myopic. India keeps alive the dream that an industrial boom is just around the corner, but does little to step up and broaden human resource development in the interim. Some business analysts fear that India will never be able to offer international companies the educated workforces found in East and Southeast Asian countries where schooling is compulsory and literacy rates high. The professions may also suffer sooner or later. A 1989 study by Delhi's independent Center for Research, Planning and Action found that by 2000 there will be significant shortages of trained people for all levels of medical services (and also in veterinary medicine), a situation perennially worsened by emigration. The survey, made for the Ministry of Science and Technology, also concluded that the total number of trained scientists and technicians, while often high in local terms, was low in comparison with the scientific workforces in industrialized countries, and that opportunities in research and development needed to be expanded if India was to meet its industrial development goals. "The political culture does not favor scientific and technical manpower," the study noted sadly. There are many needs, and there are many talented people, as Indian emigres have amply proved in every industrialized nation where they settle. At home the missing link is education. Yet many middle class Indians, whose lives are made infinitely easier by the existence of a vast servant population, will argue that independent India has done all that is necessary to give opportunities to the poor.

Anyone who lives in India or travels even for short periods in its villages and towns can see how much human energy and heartbreaking hope is squandered across the overpopulated countryside. At daybreak, bone-thin men and women are the first out on the streets, walking, cycling, or racing to leap on a swaying bus with passengers already spilling out of its doors. Under a bridge, a man emerges from a foul hut neatly dressed and strides away on his pipestem legs, head high and eyes alight, looking as if today will be the day his fortune will change. In the evening, when he returns exhausted and hollow-eyed, old men and boys are pushing heavy carts through traffic to their places among the army of vendors selling sliced fruit or fried snacks or almost anything else they think someone might want while out on a stroll. All day long, women work the fields, sweep gutters, carry construction materials, or peddle newspapers at street corners, their tiny children left on the curb in a cloud of exhaust fumes to fend for themselves. Children are everywhere: begging, selling, stealing, tending livestock, working in match factories and food-processing plants, rolling cigarettes, weaving carpets, delivering tea, scrounging for garbage when long-haul trains arrive at city terminals.

In villages and along city back streets where servants' quarters are found, poor children do not have toys. More often than not, they have jobs instead. When on festival occasions we gave toys to Neeraj and Neethi, the preschool children of the man who cleaned our house, they looked at them respectfully but were never sure what to do with them; these objects (toys made in India for Indian middle class children) had no obvious function. But when I carried a tray of snacks to the garden for guests one evening and offered some along the way to little Neethi, who was about three, she immediately assumed I was asking her to help, and reached for the tray to pass it around herself.

Almost invariably, children encountered in villages or towns are bright-eyed, alert, extremely inquisitive, and full of heartrending dreams—like Toofan, who was ten when I met him, living on a platform at New Delhi railway station and attending an informal school on an upper roof terrace of the local police substation. The school was financed by a fund set up by the film director Mira Nair from the proceeds of her movie on Bombay street children, *Salaam Bombay!* There are many thousands if not millions of children in India forced to fend for themselves on the streets, some of them orphaned, many out of touch with families they cannot telephone or write to: electronic communications and the postal service are largely out of the reach of the illiterate poor.

"I'm learning my alphabet," said Toofan, the name of an express train that he adopted for himself. He added with satisfaction that he was managing to earn about a dollar a day carrying small suitcases. "When I learn something more I will go and look for good work and lead a decent life. I want to be a doctor. How do I do that?"

His buddy, sixteen-year-old Bhagwan, another homeless boy, was more subdued; he's had more experience. "I ran away from home in Orissa years back to get some money. My family had none. I went to Howrah first. There I got on a train and came to Delhi. I got a job working in Noida [an industrial area] carrying mud on construction sites. I worked a year, but they never gave me my pay. So I came here to the station. I work eight to ten hours a day now, and get a little money. I try to save some for clothes, but somehow there is never enough. The kulis [porters] beat us a lot, because we take their work. I've been in jail twice. Once I spent two months in Tihar jail [a high-security prison] with criminals. We were given only dry bread and vegetables that had gone bad. They hit us all the time. Then I got out and came here. It took me two days to walk across Delhi from Tihar because I had no food and my stomach hurt. I was rolling around with hunger. When I'm very hungry now, I don't know what to do, so I just go to sleep. I don't see much of anything ahead in life for me."

Swami Agnivesh is a former state government official in Haryana who donned religious robes (albeit glamorous-looking, self-styled ones) and now devotes his life to organizing bonded laborers and helping indentured children. Like most dedicated people in nongovernmental social services, he assumes official statistics are unreliable at best, especially on the plight of Indian children. But using both government figures and those compiled by independent research organizations, he has calculated that the child labor force in India probably numbers about 120 million boys and girls under fourteen years of age. "Fifty-five million of these are children working more than twelve hours a day earning their own bread," he said. "About 10 million are living in slave-like conditions. Some are branded with hot irons and forced to work up to eighteen hours a day. For some children, being born into some castes guarantees they will be bonded labor for life. Certain castes are condemned to slavery. I compare this with apartheid.

"We have child labor laws," he said, "and India is the greatest champion of democracy and human rights. But if you look behind the reality, under our facade of democracy we are the biggest violator of human rights in the world. Indian spiritual leaders are not concerned about these gross inequalities. Religion has failed this country. Politics has failed this country. Even democracy has failed this country."

6

On the Playing Fields
of India

VISHWANATH PRATAP SINGH had been prime minister for nine stormy months when he took a break from the caste violence and political intrigues of New Delhi to visit the southern city of Madras, where he was welcomed as a hero by a friendly state government led by a party with its origins in an anti-Brahmin movement. On the way back, in his modest but comfortable Boeing 737 of the Indian Air Force's VIP fleet, the prime minister (who would be hounded out of office in less than two months) reflected on India's obsession with politics and the consequent politicization of every aspect of public life. I had asked him about sports; one of his ministers had become involved in an unseemly squabble over which of two rival national Olympic organizations with different party affiliations represented India at the 1990 Asian Games. Why should sports not be left to athletes?

"Yes, yes, there is too much of politics in us," he said, veering off into a more general look at culture. "Or you may say that politicians hog too much of our attention, while efforts in other sides of life, contributions in other areas, do not find the recognition they should. The limelight our politicians get our artists don't get, our writers don't get, our scientists don't get. At least our sports get publicity, a page in every newspaper. But I think we must correct this to balance life in our country." He looked out the window of the plane flying north over the Vindhyas, the mountains that separate placid South India from the turbulent upper reaches populated by his enemies. We turned to more pressing issues.

For the hapless outsider browbeaten daily with reminders that this is a four-thousand-year-old culture too arcane for Western understanding, sports offers an easy way into the web, a kind of metaphor for the larger society. All of Indian life is here—or not here, which is the point. Out of a nation that will have a billion people at the turn of the century, a nation of strapping Punjabis, fleet-footed Keralites, sinewy, desert-bred Rajasthanis, adventurous Gujaratis, and tireless mountain dwellers with lungs and legs of steel—why can't India field an Olympic team that brings home more than scandal? Where is India on the playing fields of the world?

During the Beijing Asian Games, newspaper readers in India were regaled with delicious gossip about the home team, which consisted of about a hundred athletes and an equal number of politicians, plus an army of observers from India's twenty-five states and a pack of reporters. Most Indian politicians, living in a nation of scarcity with economic and bureaucratic restraints on foreign travel, seem to regard all-expenses-paid trips abroad as an important perk of office. Sporting events are the best, because there are no seminars to attend or jobs to do.

Vijayalakshmi Pandit, Nehru's sister and a former Indian ambassador to the United Nations, reminisced in a conversation before her death at the age of ninety about the thrill of representing India abroad in its early days of independence and the sense of commitment people felt when joining the Congress Party. Membership meant more than a ticket to better living or a junket.

"Gradually, you know, things went down," she said. "Today, you go to the U.N. for a foreign jaunt. Today, we have a sort of, I'll join you, but what will you give me? attitude. We know that if we join Congress, we can get a big salary in Parliament and many other things, like trips abroad. I think we are at rock bottom now and can't go any lower. In Gandhiji's day, he touched a man, and however crude and uneducated he was, that man rose because there was a cause to which he was dedicated. Today there are no causes. Causes make you great."

At the Beijing Asian Games, the political squad provided most of the action, as it had at the Seoul Olympics in 1988, where it dominated the field in shopping and groping at hostesses. In Beijing, India won one gold medal, in *kabaddi,* a local game of team tag that looks a lot like the scramble for tickets at Delhi's train stations during peak hours. China won 126 golds.

As always, the Indian team came home to recrimination and a great deal of retrospective advice. It was observed, for example, how much better China had done in women's sports. India had two world-class female runners at the time: P. T. Usha, who was out of shape and performed disappointingly, bringing home three Asian silvers instead of the four golds she won in 1986; and Shiny Abraham, who was pregnant and had to miss Beijing altogether. In the 1992 Barcelona Olympics, India was shut out entirely, failing to win a hoped-for place in at least field hockey. A *Times of India* columnist suggested sarcastically that Indian teams might do better if there were competitions in "bottom pinching, dowry extracting, wife beating and bride burning."

The early 1990s was an appropriate time to start looking at the dearth of facilities and lack of incentives for women. The 1991 census was soon to underline how bad things were for India's female population by finding that the ratio of women to men in the country was at its lowest point in a century, about 929 women to 1,000 men. Women's organizations, demographers of both sexes, and several United Nations agencies pointed to the entrenched societal discriminations against women: the aborting of female fetuses, female infanticide, inferior nutrition of girl babies, high illiteracy and a low level of education for girls and women in India's most populous and rapidly growing northern states. About 12 million girls are born each year in India; 25 percent of them are dead by the age of fifteen. According to UNICEF, the United Nations children's organization, 300,000 fewer Indian boys than girls die annually because male children do not suffer the same neglect and discrimination.

The nineteenth-century Hindu reformer Swami Vivekananda, who was impressed on a visit to the United States with the esteem enjoyed by American women and the extent of their participation in public life, said on his return to India that a nation that does not respect women could not become great. The ancient sage and lawgiver Manu, certainly no feminist, had put it pithily: "Where women are respected, there the gods delight; and where they are not, there all works and efforts come to naught."

Sportswriters and others forced to assess one sporting disgrace after another note that athletic facilities are often equally bad for boys who might have the talent for international competition. They say that few Indian communities have recreational areas and that there are no real national farm team systems, talent spotters, or special programs for would-be athletes. Schools put little emphasis on sports or physical fitness in a country where a third of the children are born malnourished and the majority get scant or no formal education at all. Indian sports figures do not attract coaches until they are already well known, when it may be too late to develop higher levels of performance.

Politicians—who now have a free hand to meddle in the arts and broadcast media too—interfere with the choices of athletes to send abroad. Sports organizations sometimes fight over the naming of coaches or captains, stalling training and demoralizing players. Foreign expertise is rarely sought, and when it is, there are unimaginable hurdles. One of the more bizarre government news releases to cross my desk in three years was an announcement that the government of India had given a "no objection" clearance to the All India Tennis Association to allow two American coaches to come to New Delhi for two weeks to conduct a tennis camp. There would be no cost to the government, the press release assured us.

Caught in many ways between East and West when there were Communist and capitalist ways of doing things, India chose from the former Soviet bloc the path of government control or regulation of national squads, but then never followed through on the rest of the package: the highly subsidized training from childhood to competitive age and the infusion of fierce nationalistic pride in fielding unbeatable international teams. At the same time, with virtually all Western-made sporting goods barred from sale (at least legally) in India to protect local manufacturers, there was no hope of generous sponsorship, capitalist style, either. Indian athletes found neither fame nor fortune.

A few months before the 1990 Asian Games, India's ninety-four-year-old dean of sportswriters, Bobby Talyarkhan, made a passionate plea in *The Illustrated Weekly of India* for the development of sportsmindedness in the country, where, he said, "only a microscopic portion of the population" took part in recreational activity. Except for the neighborhood pickup cricket matches, played in the streets with sticks and tennis balls, the middle-class jogs or morning walks, and golfing for the rich, Indians do not have many opportunities for active play outside a few resort areas. There are no neighborhood tennis courts, bowling alleys, or roller rinks, and virtually no light-exercise entertainments like miniature golf, croquet, or boating in most Indian towns and villages. Skiing on snow or water is prohibitively expensive.

Demand as well as supply is a factor, however. Talyarkhan made the interesting observation that Indians are on the whole poor team players and that they much prefer and excel in individual competition that tests mental skills and psychological strengths—tennis, billiards, snooker, or chess, for example. "Sometimes I think that India is thoroughly inclined to those pursuits which require more than power, more brain than brawn," he said.

Bobby Talyarkhan then turned inevitably to that old bugbear: politics. "The trouble here, very frankly, is that everything is in the hands of government. It is absolutely baffling—how can politicians alone know all there is to know about every sport, so that they allocate funds, give clearances, choose teams, decide who should go to Moscow or Los Angeles or Seoul? If it's not ministers, it's some semi-official agency. Beats me, the whole business. What is the meaning of such a preposterous state of affairs? What does the future hold for Indian sports? Nothing at all. What we require is a revolution."

The Indian Army Sports Control Board has taken an interest in this national problem, offering to cooperate with the Sports Authority of India in training a few thousand adolescent boys as cadets at military sports facilities. The army, which has its own sports college at Pune, plans to offer young trainees the possibility of eventually securing a place in the noncommissioned officers' corps. While the intentions of the concerned army officers (some of them former national sports champions) are not questioned, the intrusion of the military into another area of civilian life disturbs some Indians, who wonder why an existing Sports Authority of India training program could not be expanded instead. If it isn't the politicians, does it have to be the army?

Coincidentally, it was at Pune, headquarters of the army's southern command as well as the location of its sports college, that an informal Indian survey found that many young people thought the army could run the country in general better than the civilians.

"Democracy is in danger," wrote the columnist Rahul Singh in *The Indian Express*, "when the people become so disillusioned with their money-grabbing, cynical political leaders that any other system, even military rule, seems better."

7

The Darshan Effect

Signing the visitors' book in the anteroom at the prime minister's South Block office one morning a few years ago, I looked at the entries those ahead of me had made in the space for declaring the purpose of the visit. There were the usual explanations: appointments or interviews. One man, however, had written simply, "My talented daughter." I imagined the gaunt, desperate father who must have owned up to this, who must have come full of hope that in these hallowed halls, someone in power would find a niche for his girl in government service. All over South Asia you see them: people with worn plastic bags protecting dog-eared diplomas and crumbling letters of recommendation, pressing forward in offices or at political rallies to petition the mighty.

In India, politics is still a game of personal relationships at many levels, a system the Nehru-Gandhi family cultivated at the expense of institutional development. With literacy low and no political advertising or open debate on television during election campaigns, candidates bring their messages directly to the people in speeches, enduring the sickly-sweet mountains of marigolds thrust around their necks in garlands and the thousands of hands reaching out to touch, to claim a moment of attention. When there are no election campaigns and no visits from the constituents' representatives in Parliament and state assemblies, local people go to them. Given the ineffectiveness of many government agencies and services in solving the myriad problems that arise in dealing with the bureaucracy, many Indians sooner or later have to take some pressing matter to a politician, the all-purpose "fixer" of Indian society. It could be a long wait for a telephone or gas or water connection, a delayed passport, need for medical care, the license to operate a business, a job in a government project, or help in getting out of a spot of legal trouble.

Indians have a social institution for this. They call it darshan. Attending a darshan, literally a "viewing," means joining a knot of petitioners, usually in the morning or evening, for an audience with the powerful figure whose help you seek, or by whom you hope at least to be noticed. Often people come for darshan only to glimpse a celebrity or demonstrate loyalty and affection, now and then with a gift of flowers. The importance of a leader can be measured by the size of the crowd that collects around his or her home, particularly on an auspicious occasion such as a birthday. Journalists use darshan time to penetrate a politician's inner sanctum in search of an interview, or to see who else is in attendance, in case a story is found lurking among the guests. It is all very informal, in that misleadingly disorganized-looking way in which many things get accomplished in India.

If the request of a petitioner is substantial, a little "contribution" to someone's political coffers always helps to secure a hearing. The bigger the favor, the higher the price, as any objective business leader will acknowledge. The biggest deals are cut in five-star hotels, the new clubs of the industrial class, where immensely important political and economic decisions are made over dinner in private suites. A parallel system of favors operates in the bureaucracy, where services are also bought and sold instead of provided freely. There are often quiet clashes between elected officials and professional members of the elite Indian Administrative Service, a successor to imperial Britain's Indian Civil Service, which is charged with running the offices of government at local level.

The disputes and standoffs between politicians and professional bureaucrats are not always over spoils, however. Administrative officers resent the growing interference of politicians in areas where they have no competence: city planning, the environment, health care, industrial regulation, and so on. If the politician is meddling for corrupt, self-serving reasons, so much the worse for the public. Environmentalists in the southern city of Hyderabad, for example, have not been able to stop the illegal construction of condominiums around the city's largest recreational lake because the builders have friends in state and national politics. In Uttar Pradesh, an industrialist told me how one of the notorious northern coal mafias—gangsters in control of the mines—has been able to keep piped gas supplies out of the glassmaking city of Firozabad by contributing heavily to local political coffers. The result of this cozy arrangement, the businessman said, is that Indian glassmakers cannot produce the best quality crystal for the international market because they cannot fire their glass compounds to the requisite high temperatures by using only coal. "And then the government tells us to make our exports competitive," he remarked. "We could be making crystal as good as the Czechs."

The atrophying of institutions in this personalized political world has been the focus of recent thinking and writing by Rajni Kothari, an advocate of the need for new democratic theories for India and the larger developing world. In his 1988 book *State against Democracy,* he wrote that the "decline and erosion of institutions places too great an emphasis on personalities, their sense of personal security and their attempts to use the public realm as an arena for resolving personal crises. In India the last several years have seen precisely this. It has been a period of rapid erosion of institutions."

With institutions weakening and challenges from grassroots movements, ethnic or religious minorities, and disaffected regions rising, Kothari thinks that a state apparatus no longer responsive to the people becomes especially dangerous. In an interview, he said that there has been "a massive increase in the repressive powers of the Indian state." In his book, he notes that these powers are used not only by the police, paramilitary forces, and troops but also by "mafia politicians, private armies of industrialists or landlords and armed lumpens employed by dominant factions or communities."

Legislators at state and national levels have the power to fix, rearrange, or control the public services because they have arrogated that authority to themselves at the expense of responsible, elected local government, that bedrock of American democracy. Local self-government has never been given scope to develop in most parts of India. The village democracies of Mahatma Gandhi's dream could have evolved through the strengthening of the indigenous system of elected local councils called panchayats—from the Sanskrit for "five wise men." Where enlightened state governments, notably in Karnataka and West Bengal, resurrected and institutionalized the panchayat system, giving towns and villages decision-making powers, local development has been quicker and more successful. But those have been the exceptions, and they are not free of problems. Bureaucrats in New Delhi or state capitals more often than not decide what is best for most Indians.

"Gandhiji wanted villages to grow their own food and make their own cloth for self-sufficiency," said Lakshmi Chand Jain, a development expert and critic of the overcentralization of government and the erosion of states' rights by the Congress Party and the Nehru dynasty. "Gandhiji wanted political, economic and social autonomy at the village level." However, Jain, winner of Asia's highest prize for public service, the Magsaysay Award, opposed Rajiv Gandhi's ill-fated 1989 bill to establish a new panchayat system because it was structured from the top down, essentially cutting out state governments and greatly circumscribing local action. Rajiv Gandhi, like his mother and predecessor, was loath to divest any of the enormous powers of the central government or to give the states more authority. Jain remarked that Rajiv's embrace of the panchayat system was something like buying a goat and then calling yourself a disciple of Mahatma Gandhi because he also kept goats.

"Gandhiji's system is now inverted," Jain said. "Why should we have food sent from Punjab to Karnataka? Why should all the cloth be made in two cities, Bombay and Ahmedabad? The center occupies all the space in planning. Unless that changes, and planning is decentralized, the panchayats will be empty boxes. Other space is occupied by the bureaucracy in villages and districts. The politicians work with them. Karnataka tried to find an answer to the knotty problem of how to get the bureaucracy to give up space so that they would not be at loggerheads with elected councils."

At Jain's suggestion, I went to Karnataka to talk with state officials and see a recently established local panchayat system at work in a rural district of Bangalore, the state capital. It had taken Ramakrishna Hegde, a former chief minister of the state, a quarter of a century to put a local government plan into action because of Congress Party opposition. Hegde was a leader of the Janata Dal, the party of Prime Minister V. P. Singh, Rajiv Gandhi's chief rival for power. When I first met Hegde, Karnataka was two and a half years into establishing local councils. Hegde was ebullient on the subject, although the Congress Party had recently engineered his ouster as chief minister on telephone-tapping charges—absurd, in that a Congress Party government in New Delhi was tapping about four hundred telephones (some of them belonging to the administration's own ministers) at the same time. Around Bangalore alone, nineteen of twenty districts had established local assemblies and village panchayats. Across the state, more than fifty-six thousand people had been elected to these bodies.

"Never in our history were such gatherings collected," Hegde said in a conversation in his home. "Everyone was an accredited representative of the people. It was such a satisfying sight. In India, the first transfer of power took place in 1947, from colonial to native rulers. But today a more significant transfer has taken place, from the rulers to the people themselves." Hegde lauded the elected assemblies and panchayats for their common sense. They had realistic goals and limited demands. "You're not going to see a village asking for a medical college," he said.

In Bangalore and in local offices in the village of Budigere, in the flat countryside north of the state capital, newly elected local representatives and civil servants who worked with them vied to tell me about their accomplishments. Every village in rural Bangalore district, enjoying the new right to decide how development money was spent, now had a school. There had been significant improvement in the quality of drinking water with the installation of hand pumps, and the incidence of epidemic gastroenteritis had been sharply reduced. In Budigere, where five women had been elected to a twenty-five-member panchayat representing fourteen small villages grouped in a local government unit called a mandal, residents showed me their new silkworm farm and their dairy. They talked about the new shopping complex they wanted to build—a row of small wooden huts, but a shopping complex nonetheless. They argued over plans for an adult literacy program, debated how to conserve soil, and discussed the shortage of electricity. "In thirty years of the old system," an old man said, "we could never have accomplished this much." A few years later, Karnataka's panchayat system was in jeopardy, again under attack from a Congress Party fearful of the dilution of its powers in the state and from politicians threatened by the concept of accountability that local government fosters.

As the population of India grows uncontrollably and scarcities mount, the need to get around the system will become ever more urgent and the power of politicians to intervene will be further enhanced. The manipulation of slum life is perhaps the most audacious political art form. When squatter settlements begin to form around any of India's cities—drawing rural people or illegal migrants from neighboring countries, especially Bangladesh—a politician or party is quick to move in to create a "vote bank." In return for a communal water tap or protection from eviction, the poor slum dwellers are expected to vote the right way whenever called on to do so (and as often as necessary on polling day if the election is close). Ward bosses keep the slum in line. Volunteers for a charity group working with children in a squatter community I once visited at Govindpuri, on the edge of New Delhi, told me that they had to be very careful to cultivate the sufferance of the political boss who didn't want competition where the provision of services was involved. There was much that could not be done, however great the need of the children condemned to that muddy, sewage-littered slum, because of political opposition. The charity persevered, however, subtly instilling in the minds of the squatters the notion that they could reduce their dependence through self-help. It is a revolutionary message.

For three years, we lived across the street in New Delhi from H. K. L. Bhagat, a former government minister and Delhi Congress Party boss who apparently thought he had the ultimate vote bank across the Jamuna River in an area being opened for new middle class suburbs. This East Delhi constituency, with a large component of slums, is now one of the most populous in India and, until 1991, it seemed to be safely Bhagat's. Nearly every day, poor people were brought into our affluent neighborhood in buses and trucks to stand outside the Bhagat compound and cheer their *netaji*, their "honorable leader." Bhagat zindabad! Long live Bhagat! These willing crowds were also useful in demonstrations, parades, and political rallies. In November 1984, some of them were called in to help decimate the Sikh neighborhoods in the Delhi metropolitan area, survivors say. All of this is part of what Indians call "Congress culture," the mode of operation of India's largest party, which also shakes down local shopkeepers for donations and uses the intelligence agencies to spy on political opponents and do opinion sampling.

The Congress Party and H. K. L. Bhagat suffered a surprisingly humiliating defeat in the East Delhi constituency in 1991, however, at the hands of the relatively new and better disciplined Bharatiya Janata Party, which had strong support in the rising middle class neighborhoods. Other parties cut

into votes of the poorer sections. The Bahujan Samaj, a party of untouchables, preached a bootstraps message. The Janata Dal of V. P. Singh brought
in its plea for more affirmative action. Voters listened to new ideas and
proved that vote banks are not forever. More seeds of change were being
sown.

8

Mixies and Marutis

THE PUNJABI FARMER on his rough cot of woven twine, his new tractor parked in a mud garage; the fashionable public relations executive in Bombay with her Western clothes, her own apartment, and her nonstop social life; the architect in Calcutta pioneering urban conservation; the computer programmer in Delhi who drives a Mercedes; the lecturer in Madras who takes the bus to save for a foreign vacation; the guru in his tax haven; and the property developer who is forever adding something to his multimillion-dollar, state-of-the-art hospital because an astrologer told him he would die when the work was completed—all of them belong to the new Indian middle class, an Asian phenomenon of gigantic proportions and innumerable contradictions.

There may be 150 million Indians who qualify as middle class now, still a minority in India but a group numerically larger than the population of most countries. Some market researchers dare to suggest that a few hundred million Indians might be included if a ticket to the middle class comes with the ability to buy an electric fan, a bicycle, or a small television set. Producers of consumer goods are dazzled by them, politicians and religious leaders court them, old-time Indian nationalists deplore them, and sociologists are just beginning to sort and fathom them. Foreign companies and investors would love to tap the extraordinary potential markets they represent. Middle class Indians are often (but not always) unashamedly materialistic in their pursuit and flaunting of affluence in a country where rumpled Gandhian asceticism was the hallmark of an older establishment.

Their favorite car is the Maruti, a fast and flashy Indian version of a

Suzuki overpriced at up to $14,000 in a country where the annual per capita gross national product is under $400. (It costs at least $1,000 just to get on the Maruti waiting list.) They love the familiar gadgets: hair driers, pressure cookers, microwaves, and electric blenders they call "mixies." They also support an ethnic design movement that, paradoxically, keeps alive the spectacular craftsmanship of traditional Indian weavers, potters, puppeteers, jewelrymakers, and folk artists of every kind. The intellectual elite hates this bourgeois "ethnic chic" fad, condemning it as a co-opting and commercializing of pure artisanship. To a neutral visitor returning to India after a decade or more away, there could be nothing more welcoming than homes stripped of their heavy pseudo-British look and filled with dhurries, pillows, giant ceramic pots, and sculptures with Indian souls, their inspiration and materials drawn from Indian land.

In the southern city of Bangalore, I met a young couple, Vikram and Smita Satyanath, who soon became my subconscious model of a new generation of middle class life. I was researching an article on Indian society that never made it into print in *The New York Times Magazine* because the editors and I were not in agreement on how to define what it means to be middle class in India at the end of the twentieth century. This was one of a number of lessons learned about how American perceptions of India can be befuddled by applying our own definitions of social and political terms to a totally different national context, especially when we are all using the English language. To observe outcastes voting at separate polling booths or the Indian paramilitary police in action, for example, is to search for a word other than democratic. When I wrote an article about how the citizens of an efficiently run company steel town in Bihar dreaded a court-ordered switch to an elected local government because of the corruption and unremitting violence of politics in the state, an editor in faraway New York wrote the headline: "Good Government Scares a Good City in India." If anyone in Jamshedpur saw the story, he or she must have been thoroughly mystified by our Western logic. The last thing in the world headed their way was good government. Not in Bihar.

When I began to explore the middle class, I was advised by many Indians whose judgment I trusted not to focus on the "movers and shakers" of Delhi or Bombay so beloved of the glossy magazines, who were either dependent on government jobs or awash in "black" money (undeclared income, often obtained illegally), which they lavished on vulgar displays like full-size plaster models of palaces for family weddings, marble swimming pools, and colonnaded homes crammed with gilded overstuffed furniture—styles variously described by acid-tongued journalists as Bania Byzantine, Punjabi Baroque, and Delhi Decadent—or spent on money-laundering shopping trips to London or Singapore. (The late columnist Dhiren Bhagat used to say it was no longer possible to get rich honestly in India.) An ordinary hardworking couple like the Satyanaths, born, raised, and educated in India in self-made families with two or three generations in the middle class, would personalize and represent more fairly a slice of a new nation struggling to emerge from the old. Or to be more accurate, one of those multiple modern middle classes forming in India, because Bangalore, while a sophisticated and upbeat city that leaves a positive impression of urban life, is not an average Indian town demographically. It is something of an Indian city of the future: a mix of religions and regions, drawing people from all over India to work in scientific and industrial research or to retire in the relatively clean air of the Deccan Plateau. It has the most modern shops and a thriving cafe and pub culture. It is also a linguistic collage reflecting a country that has at least fifteen official languages and 1,642 regional dialects.

The Satyanaths met backstage at a theater in Madras. She was a volunteer stagehand and he was Atahualpa in an amateur production of *Royal Hunt of the Sun*. They were in their twenties, and both had begun careers in advertising. Three years later the stagehand and the actor got married. No marriage brokers. No family interference. No astrologers. No dowry. Just two young and energetic Indians making their own way through life. They don't think of themselves as unusual, but a lot about the life they lead runs counter to Indian tradition. In their early thirties, they were living alone with their small son, Siddharth, in a modest apartment when we met. No relatives in residence. No live-in servants. No puja room or family shrine, although they are Hindus. When the baby was born, Vikram took a month off to learn to care for him. Like the unpublicized, unsung majority of middle class Indians, Vikram and Smita can live comfortably on just under $500 a month, a good salary in India, supplemented by company-subsidized rent. But they are not rich. Going out for ice cream is a social event. A lot of young Americans would feel at home with them.

"We have built our house from scratch, from having nothing at all," said Smita. "Right from collecting drawing room furniture, to beds, to the dining room table, to the fridge. We started with a black and white TV, which was second-hand, and then we got a color TV. Now we have a VCR. We planned all this out. We save for a period and get what we want. We used to go around on a motorbike at first," she said. He added: "It was a 1970 Jawa, a Czechoslovakian bike, because that's what we could afford in those days. Our first car was an old Fiat—1960. We got a Maruti in 1989, also second hand."

"We are in a profession where there seems to be some kind of scarcity of talent, and so perhaps we have, in terms of money earned, grown faster than other members of the middle class," said Vikram. At the top of his profession, he might look forward to a salary of about $20,000 a year. Vikram and Smita and their friends, living outside the orbit of the large and often claustrophobic extended family, revel in spontaneous social events. Entertaining at home is still the norm in a country only beginning to develop a restaurant culture and a disposable income to sustain it, even in cosmopolitan Bangalore.

"Depending on the city, partying and meeting up with a small group of people on a regular basis is a very common thing," said Vikram, the son of a tea broker and a school principal who was educated at the innovative Mayo College, a secondary school in Ajmer, and then at the Jesuits' Loyola College in Madras. "Drinking together would be a common thing. Watching movies together would be a common thing." Salon evenings are an inexpensive form of entertainment. "I've been talking to someone who says let's have a session on great relatively unknown Hollywood actors," Vikram said. "He thinks someone like Robert Mitchum is the master of nonacting. I don't know why he said this, but it sounded interesting enough. So I said, OK, I'll put together a bunch of ten people at home and you explain your reasons why. Tell us, what is nonacting? There's another chap who says, let's have a session on Pink Floyd before it broke up—on their music and evolution and things like that."

Vikram, who has in his spare time acted in works by Thornton Wilder, Edward Albee, Tom Stoppard, and Werner Fassbinder, as well as in Indian plays strong on social commentary, made his first trip to New York a few years ago with Smita, where they said they really couldn't find any shows worth seeing, on or off Broadway. They were more impressed with the range of music available, and made the rounds of clubs where they could hear contemporary sounds. Smita, who has a brother living in New Jersey, discovered suburban shopping malls. A creative artist, she came back wanting to try her hand at designing clothes for export.

With a diversity of new careers to choose from in private industry and professions like advertising, marketing, and the luxury hotel and tourist business, many young Indians like these are turning their backs on the traditional goal of a career in government or politics. Officials say that India's best and brightest can no longer be counted on to apply for the prestigious Indian Foreign Service or its domestic counterparts, especially the Indian Administrative Service, although there will never be a serious shortage of applicants for berths in the IAS. This elite club of about 5,000 men and women in the IAS and the officer corps of the Indian Police, Customs, Revenue, Railways, and other federal services are expected to run India. More than 100,000 Indians apply to join each year, competing for only 700 annual openings. Apart from a lifetime income with housing and numerous other privileges, a young man or woman joining the IAS or another national service corps can expect to marry better when the family begins negotiating to find a spouse. The qualification is listed in those marriage ads, along with the promise of a "wheatish" or fair complexion, wherever possible. Indians persist in their obsession with skin color.

The movement into private industry, advertising media, and the think tanks assumes, of course, a continually expanding economy. Prospects for that are clouded if India does not act decisively to cut its population growth, improve infrastructure, and increase energy supplies. Indian entrepreneurs need working telephones and post offices where mail is not routinely opened and often pilfered. They need the freedom to dispatch samples abroad without hours and days of debate with postal clerks or courier companies over what items can and cannot be sent out of India. For years, articles of clothing had to be scissored (and therefore rendered unwearable) for export clearance. Customs officials have the right to stop any package of photographs if the pictures are deemed to contain something unflattering to the national image, as a leading photographer in Calcutta discovered when he tried to submit a portfolio of his city for an exhibition abroad. The DHL office in Bombay told me that I could not dispatch news photographs because the United States forbade the importing of all pictures, a ridiculous claim apparently proffered to dissuade me from putting the courier service through the paperwork mill. No reasonably aware Indian would trust a valuable gift to the postal or courier services; an acquaintance in Delhi told me that he always sent duplicate invitations to parties in the hope that one would reach its destination. "This shouldn't happen" has been replaced by "You shouldn't have done that" when someone is victimized in this ethically flaccid bureaucratic society, Gunnar Myrdal's "soft state." The fault is yours, dummy, for trusting the system.

Vikram and Smita Satyanath and their friends are representative of a generation weary of traditional politics and politicians, who have allowed India to sink into inefficiency and corruption while perennially vowing that life is getting better. "The whole problem is that there is a lot of talk, but we don't have much time," said Vikram. "India doesn't have much time." Significantly, the Satyanaths, secular and cosmopolitan in outlook, were willing to consider the right-wing Bharatiya Janata Party. "We've tried the others and they haven't done much," Vikram said. "Even though the BJP has some kind of Hindu image and I am reasonably secular, they seem to have a clear-cut program and I would be willing to vote for that."

India's impatient, more affluent young are on a swing into social iconoclasm not unlike that of the American '60s generation. A lecturer at Mt. Carmel College, an expensive and highly selective women's college in Bangalore, asked her students in 1990 to rank fifteen things that were "in" or "out" among their peers. The results were published in the college newspaper, aptly named For Now! These were declared "out": wearing spectacles, honesty, being just housewives, idealism, Indian music, reading literary classics, carrying textbooks to class, studying for exams, watching educational or meaningful movies, narrow-minded parents, helping with housework, hard work and diligence, arranged marriages, religion, and non-participation in politics. The sometimes-contradictory "in" list ranked what was fashionable this way: ethnic clothes and going punk, bunking (cutting classes), premarital and extramarital affairs, divorce, slang, four-letter words, voting, makeup and fashion jewelry, love marriages, sex and violence in movies, higher education, eating chocolate fudge, women working, women smoking and drinking, and bright colors.

"The young are more worldly, more practical, less idealistic," said Professor Leela Rao at Bangalore University. "They're ready for anything." In Indian cities, young middle class women are for the first time abandoning in significant numbers the traditional Indian sari for dresses, jeans, or the North Indian costume of baggy trousers and long blouse known as the salwar-kamiz. Smita Satyanath, who says she "can't move around in a sari," saves them for formal occasions. In Calcutta, Alka Verma—Indian administrator for a novel Washington-based program for small-scale innovators in development called the Ashoka fellowships—uses her spare time to design fashionably cut salwar-kamiz outfits for office wear. These swinging tunics with padded shoulders over softly gathered harem pants are snapped up by eager clients. Apart from flattering the Indian female figure with its narrow shoulders and broad bottom, Verma said, the comfortable suits cover the midriff skin that saris expose and office Casanovas pinch. Fashion in some Indian cities seems to be changing far more rapidly than among Indian communities abroad. At a horse race in Bombay, I counted more skirts and trousers than saris in the members' enclosure at the city's fashionable Mahalaxmi racetrack.

There are other middle class Indias, more traditional than this, and sometimes they are in collision with the world of the urban bourgeoisie. In the small village of Hasanpur, in the northern state of Haryana, barely forty miles from New Delhi, farming families of the sturdy Jat caste were watching with some concern as fertile land around them was being bought for the weekend "farmhouses" of the urban upper middle class. Jats form a sub-caste that has enjoyed a meteoric rise through the green revolution in agriculture. Many Jat farmers have become rich themselves; the crossroads towns of Haryana have shops brimming over with consumer goods. In Hasanpur, where about 360 families lived, there were few shops, but there were sturdy houses built along unpaved streets, where plump bullocks were tied. Hasanpur enjoyed a good deal of social and financial security. Its residents spoke with the shrewd good sense of most Indian villagers. When they described the new "farmhouses" over the hill, they used the English word, though all the conversation was in their Haryanvi dialect: the newcomers were seen as impostors, strangers playing at rural life, and their dwellings with irrigated lawns and swimming pools didn't qualify to be called farmhouses in the local language.

"The people of the city are dying of suffocation and come here for good, clean air," explained Pratap Singh, resting after the end of the harvest sea-son in the town square with his friends, all sitting on walls or the ubiquitous string cots called charpoys. "But there is something ominous about this. We still don't understand what will happen here. We know that this building of farmhouses for city people is not going to lead to employment for us, except as caretakers. We would rather have a factory."

"Oh, they come and hire our bullock carts on weekends for 100 rupees, so they can climb up and be photographed," he said, to a roar of laughter all around. "Trouble is, people are selling their agricultural land for the money. But when the money—and the land—are gone, what do they have?" Resentment against the urban middle class runs high in many rural communities where farmers say that cities are consuming too large a share of government revenue, natural resources, and energy, while the country's food producers are neglected. In Hasanpur, electricity was available for only a few hours each night; air conditioners hummed round the clock in Delhi. The farmers had been up to town and seen this for themselves. They also had taken note of the markups in the prices of their produce in city markets, and wondered why those big profit margins should go to someone else. Farmers, however, pay no taxes on agricultural income, and enjoy subsidies in both buying supplies and selling goods. Many have learned to play the critical food market, withholding supplies from government procurement centers and the bazaars until the price is right.

Unlike many other nations that became independent since World War II, India did not have to create a middle class, rural or urban. Under British administration, a corps of Indian civil servants kept the offices of empire running. (Years ago someone told me a joke about how South India had produced so many typists that a whole new subcaste had emerged called Remington.) There were also the mercantile babus, traders who amassed fortunes and acquired status dealing with imperial Britain and other Western nations, including the young United States. And there were the powerful indigenous industrial families who had played important parts in economic, social, and political development for the greater part of a century before independence. By the time Mahatma Gandhi began his nonviolent freedom movement against the British, manufacturing houses such as the Tatas, Birlas, and Bajaj group had led the way in establishing a strong capitalist base. They also contributed generously to Indian nationalism and, after independence, established think tanks, medical centers, and research organizations in the public interest. The Tata research institutes in energy, medicine, and the social sciences continue to produce some of the most reliable, best documented surveys of India.

Govinda Pillai, a Communist Party intellectual in the southern state of Kerala and director of the state's Film Development Corporation under a leftist government, said that the presence at independence of this influential home-grown middle class made it impossible for the Indian left to capture the independence movement in India, as Communists under Ho Chi Minh succeeded in doing in Vietnam or radical movements did in the former Portuguese colonies in Africa.

"We actually wanted to have a revolution," Pillai recalled in a conversation in his office in the Kerala state capital, Trivandrum, since renamed Thiruvananthapuram for the sake of historical purity. "We actually had some liberated areas, where we opened schools and began land reform. But Indian Communists made one serious miscalculation: we underestimated the strength of the Indian bourgeoisie." Ironically, Indian Communism, with its limited appeal to the entrepreneurial middle class, would also be unable to build a mass base among the rural poor, or make any other impact on the countryside, where caste and family loyalties were strong and millions of independent peasant farmers showed no proclivity for collective agriculture. Communism was destined to remain an urban intellectual force, largely the preserve of a highly educated, well-born elite, a few of its leaders converted to the cause at Cambridge University, where in the 1930s, '40s, and '50s they encountered the fashionable British Left and the Stalinist Soviet agents who manipulated it.

Other Indians were deeply influenced by the Fabian socialists of the London School of Economics and the later neo-socialists of Sussex University. Their equally anti-capitalist (and therefore often anti-American) views shaped important economic, social and foreign policies in the early years of Indian independence. Although the industrial sector, until it began to benefit handsomely from protectionism, and the kulaks of the countryside were not enthusiastic about socialism, leftist opinions did pervade the thinking of the early intellectual-academic middle class, leaving a disproportionately large impression on the universities and mainstream political movements.

A less ideological atmosphere is just beginning to pervade academic life as India moves toward the twenty-first century. With the United States replacing Britain (which no longer subsidizes Commonwealth students) as the preferred destination of Indians studying abroad, and with science, technology, and the advertising and marketing world drawing bright young men and women away from politicized liberal arts or social science courses, there are more refreshingly open youthful minds among the under-forties. Uprisings against Communist regimes worldwide have exposed leftist utopias for what most of them were: repressive, intolerant societies. Rajiv Gandhi volunteered in an interview that the Fabian socialism of his grandfather's circle was "out," along with the leftist-inspired nationalization-raj of his mother's regime. "Socialism proved to be economically not very viable," he said, with uncharacteristic understatement.

Rajiv Desai, an American-educated journalist who now heads the Indian Public Affairs Network, a public relations company, packages his history of recent social changes compactly. "In the 1950s and 1960s," he said, "there used to be three classes in India: the poor, the rich and the privileged intelligentsia, who had the privileges of the rich and the resources of the poor—I call them the priviligentsia. The rich and poor were the class system, which fit in beautifully with Fabian socialism. The priviligentsia—largely the government's administrative and foreign services—was a modern avatar of a caste system. Now, these new middle class guys have come along to challenge both the class-based and caste-based structure of India, and they are threatening to cause turmoil."

For instance, they want travel abroad made easier. They want the right to hold international credit cards. They want more business class seats on otherwise nightmarish domestic flights and the right to buy themselves other comforts when traveling, Desai says. Why should these people who are expected to work hard to develop India be relegated to the shabby steam-room airport lounges when today's priviligentsia—the politicians and high officials of government—enjoy free seats, air-conditioned lounges, fawning service, and the power to delay flights and bump paying passengers?

"It's a real, honest-to-goodness middle class that's emerging, the kind that spawned the Benettons of this world, the ones who wear the T-shirts that say 'I love Delhi,' " said Desai. "The rich in their old British-style clubs hate them because they are seen as upstarts. The poor hate them because they are seen as opportunists. And the priviligentsia hate them because of their conspicuous consumption."

In a country where barely half of the people are literate and half live in severe poverty and have little power, the middle classes, while still a minority, are gaining a lockhold on agriculture, education, communications, information, and scientific technologies, the tools by which they can reshape their society in their own image. That image, while still kaleidoscopically fragmented, is gradually coming into focus as Indian. Not Punjabi or Bengali or Gujarati first, but Indian. Advertising is speeding the process and may prove to be the country's most effective unifier, says Father Joe Naidu, at the Media Center in Bangalore, run by Indian Jesuits. The center trains journalists and operates a design consultancy and sound and video studios, all booming new fields of expertise. Advertising is creating pan-Indian tastes, common images for the young and transregional consumer desires, he says. As it grows into a respected profession, advertising spawns experts in the press and research organizations who are learning new ways to chart social development in India by looking at what and how much people are purchasing, or are being urged to buy. Selling by brand name on television, billboards, or in glossy magazines began with soaps and toiletries and some basic foods, and branched into motorbikes, household appliances, decorator bathroom fixtures, fashionable clothes, and condoms, including a brand called Kama Sutra. Soft drinks and snack foods are also pushed aggressively. Hard drinks present a problem, however, since they cannot be advertised. Inventive Indians get around that by sleight of hand, packaging ice-cube molds or snacks in boxes identical to those containing whiskey, gin, or rum bottles. At first glance, the full-page picture of two young people setting up dinner around a campfire, glasses in hand, seems to be a portrait of drink time, with the name of a well-known whiskey on the box in the foreground. The text is pretty explicit: "Alone in the wilderness. Enjoying their togetherness. The night is for sizzling barbecues. And it's time for cocktails." But look again. There is an asterisk by the word "cocktails," referring to this message in minuscule print at the bottom of the page: "Cocktail: Preparation of food, esp. as appetizer."

While many intellectuals regard consumer advertising as an obscenity in a country where a majority of people live beyond the reach of the consumer society, most Indians agree that concepts like brand recognition or purchasing for the sake of image-building are widely understood, down to village level. Leela Rao, the Bangalore University film professor, says that young people watch TV and films not so much out of a search for information but out of a new consumer awareness. Many are tempted to buy luxuries they see, using recently eased credit plans they cannot really afford. "Often income hasn't grown much; they're just having more things," she said, cautioning me against taking a superficial view of middle class affluence. "It is very difficult to say what the middle class is if you define it by the goods people have. Income would be a better guide than consumer items owned." Her hunches are backed by more recent research, which shows that in some product areas—notably color television and large appliances—sales are actually declining and prices rising. Neither should be happening if the demands of the potential middle class consumer market are in fact as large or unlimited as analysts had predicted. The decade of the 1990s will test the real spending power of Indians when the initial consumer boom recedes.

Whatever the economic trend, the new uses the middle classes are making of the media will inevitably alter politics in India, says the social scientist Ashis Nandy. "Old or new, the Indian middle classes are entering into an interesting phase, in the sense that they have begun flexing their political muscle in a way that would have been unthinkable fifteen years ago," he said in an interview at Delhi's liveliest think tank, the Center for the Study of Developing Societies. "Technically, in terms of proportions, urban India is not large—less than one-fourth of the entire country. But in absolute terms, urban India, where much of the middle class lives, is enormous, larger than three-fourths of the countries that are members of the United Nations. This huge size, combined with certain kinds of skills that are available within that sector, combined again with an open political system, gives this new middle class a clout that has begun to change the political face of society. The older political linkages based on caste, region and religion still exist, but they have to coexist with an altogether different set of categories where images, mediagenicity, slogans, and all the paraphernalia of mass political culture— or the mass culture of contemporary politics—have begun to play a much more important role."

There are negative sides to the middle class phenomenon. One of the most tragic in its irony is the increase in the barbaric practice of bride-burning. It begins with dowry, one of those concepts from another age that contemporary India seems unable or unwilling to discard. Collecting a dowry for a daughter was once a father and mother's way to insure that she would have some property of her own in the days when Hindu women had no right of inheritance, an inequality rectified by law in 1951. In marriage, the daughter would take her dowry—often the bulk of it in gold jewelry and silk saris—to her husband's home. Her ornaments were hers to treasure and enjoy, or use in time of crisis, and her husband had no right to them. Somewhere along the line, dowry got converted into a twisted version of wergeld, a heartlessly calculated (and illegal) price demanded by a man and his family for the privilege of allowing a young woman to take him away in marriage.

When two families get down to negotiating a marriage, particularly if the woman and her parents stand to gain status from the match, the husband-to-be gets out his shopping list. Perhaps he asks for the rupee equivalent of a few thousand dollars and a refrigerator, a color television, or a motorbike. That would not be unusual. The more brazen, seduced by the sudden prospects offered by a newly materialistic culture, demand a Swiss watch—usually a Rolex—or a luxury car and hundreds of thousands of rupees, along with the usual gold jewelry and clothes. A woman becomes equal to the value of the goods her parents can turn over to her in-laws. Some girls never get this far: they commit suicide as teenagers rather than see their parents impoverished and humiliated in the dowry negotiations that lie ahead. Others move on to the next hurdle, marriage and a new life in their in-laws' home. As prospective brides, they may be forced to parade before a suitor's family to be tested for feminine charms and graces. In Lucknow's best hotel one afternoon, I watched this ritual in the public lobby. In front of total strangers, the young woman, waiting for the arrival of the putative bride-groom's clan, was fussed over by her female relatives, who adjusted the pleats of her sari again and again, rearranged her jewelry and her hair, and snapped at her when she uncrossed her carefully placed hands. She was a picture of misery. When the young man and his family arrived, she dropped her head and began to fidget, to the harsh glares of her mother. In more conservative families and in Muslim communities, the young woman and man are unlikely to meet at all before they are thrown together into the marriage bed and bond. When I asked a Muslim father whose son's wedding I was attending whether the young man hadn't wanted at least to meet his future wife once before agreeing to marry her, the older man replied: "That wouldn't be necessary. We know his tastes."

Women who are fighting to stop the abuse of brides say that from the start of her marriage, the new member of the family suffers humiliation at her mother-in-law's hands. That is also traditional; the bride is expected to earn respect by serving her new family faithfully and selflessly. The young woman is frequently denied the privacy to get to know her husband, who may feel no tenderness or protectiveness toward her because he has not chosen to marry her for love. It is commonly known among Indian women that marital sex more often begins in rape than in mutual passion. Lucky couples grow to love and care for each other as time goes by, and often the relationship becomes extremely close and strong. But when things go wrong, the slide into tragedy can be precipitous. A dissatisfied new husband may decide the dowry wasn't big enough, and dun or blackmail the bride's parents for more. He may beat his wife, abetted by his mother and other family members. In the end, he may decide to get rid of her and find another wife with a better dowry. He can't send her home and bring on the shame and expense of divorce. The easy way out is to kill her and tell the police that she died in an accident or committed suicide. So common is the syndrome that such murders are known generically as dowry deaths. A criminal investigation is mandated when any young woman dies suspiciously in the first seven years of marriage, whether or not dowry is involved, the New Delhi police told me when I decided to investigate for myself one of those one-paragraph newspaper reports about a reported "suicide." In this case, the woman, Rani Singh, had endured more than five years of domestic violence in a marriage in which the size of dowry was never an issue, her relatives told me.

Of course the majority of Indian marriages—arranged or not, with or without dowry—do not degenerate into this kind of violence. But in an upper middle class neighborhood of New Delhi called Chittaranjan Park, Bani Dasgupta, the leader of a self-help group for women, said that "in every tenth house there is a problem." The figure was as shocking to them as to any outsider because the neighborhood had been settled primarily by Bengali-speaking Hindus from what is now Muslim-dominated Bangladesh, and Bengalis do not have a reputation for domestic violence or the systematic denigration of women. When another reporter and I met Dasgupta she was preparing for a memorial service. A sixty-five-year-old woman, Subprapha Banerjee, had been murdered after she refused to move from the family home that her estranged husband had sold without her consent. It was the second case of apparent homicide that the Samati had encountered in the neighborhood in a few months. Earlier, the charred body of twenty-three-year-old Suparna Sen Sharma had been delivered by taxi to a local hospital. Suparna's two-year-old daughter told the police that she had last seen her mother in a dark room being given "medicine" by grandma. "Mama bitten by snake," the little girl said. Neighbors, who had comforted the weeping Suparna on previous occasions, heard her scream the night she died and tried to get into the house, only to be chased away by Suparna's in-laws. The neighborhood, which fought to deny the husband's family bail for four months, is convinced that Suparna was poisoned, then burned.

The danger to the bride is enhanced by her inability to flee to her parents' home because of logistics—Suparna's family was in Calcutta, on the other side of India—or by the social disgrace this would cause. Pramila Dandavate, a leading advocate of women's rights, urges parents to abandon their embarrassment or inhibitions about welcoming home a young woman in obvious distress and give a daughter shelter until they feel she is reasonably safe. Sending her back to an abusive husband can be signing her death warrant. In Chittaranjan Park, Bani Dasgupta thinks that the most potent weapons other women have in combating domestic violence are social pressure and publicity. Members of her group have reported a civil servant to his government superior and embarrassed him in his workplace. They have cornered a woman with an influential, high-profile job and confronted her with proof that she was abusing her daughter-in-law, whose young husband was studying abroad.

When a bride dies, her end usually comes horribly, in the kind of "kitchen fire," made to look accidental or suicidal, in which Suparna Sen Sharma perished. Thousands of Indian women die this way annually, doused in kerosene. Not infrequently, they are drugged, poisoned, or knocked unconscious first. When Rani Singh died in a ball of flames in a tiny house in a civil servants' compound in New Delhi in December 1988, her cousin told me that her three little children slept through the immolation. There were apparently no screams.

"On that day," her cousin said, as we sat in the little house a few days later, "my uncle had gone to see her to see if she was happy. She had been unhappy in the past because her husband, a drunkard, always beat her. But later her husband went out and took wine. He came home later at night, and they had a fight over milk, who would buy the milk. At about 11:30 in the night her husband went to a neighbor's house and told the gentleman there: My wife is burning. The man came and saw that she was on fire, and knew that she was already dead. Only Rani was burning, nothing else in the room. No one heard her cry. In our opinion, we think that her husband murdered her first and then threw the kerosene over her body and set her alight."

No one has comprehensive national figures on such deaths, but women's rights organizations and neighborhood support groups believe the total number, extrapolated from statistics in states where feminist organizations are actively monitoring the trend, is steadily rising toward the tens of thousands. As India grows more modern, it also grows more uncivilized in the most intimate of human relations, a gruesome confluence of half-understood new ideas and base instincts called up from some primeval past. Nothing epitomized this more grotesquely that the reports of the wealthy man in New Delhi who poured an expensive brand of imported scotch over his wife before lighting the match. Pramila Dandavate calls the perpetrators of these atrocities "feudal beings influenced by a materialistic attitude." She said that at the root of the problem was the low regard Indian society, at least North

Indian society, had for girls and women. "Basically, we don't believe that people are equal," she said. "Contact with Western culture has made us only greedy," she went on. "Meanwhile, we are losing our sense of justice. We have not preserved our old cultures, nor are we prepared to accept the equality of the Western culture whose materialism we imitate."

Another side of the middle class phenomenon that worries many Indians is the courting of the rising bourgeoisie by the extreme Hindu right. Hindu militancy panders to more regressive, populist and superstitious uses of the majority religion, including the denigration of women and tolerance for *sati*, the illegal practice of burning a woman on her husband's funeral pyre. The Bharatiya Janata Party, heavily supported by shopkeepers and owners of small businesses (often combining upper caste birth and middle class milieu), is now leading the challenge against the first two of Jawaharlal Nehru's four pillars of Indian polity: secularism, socialism, nonalignment, and democracy. While this is to some extent part of a larger wave of revisionism questioning or seeking to rectify the Nehruvian (and to some extent Gandhian) legacies which have left India so poor and vulnerable, the highly disciplined Hindu revivalists have other, less constructive agendas. They appeal to people uprooted by urbanization and swiftly changing lifestyles with the promise of a strong personal and national identity couched in chauvinistically Hindu terms, at the expense of minority rights and viewpoints. They offer status and pride in Hinduism to both upper caste Hindus and those on the rise from lower socioeconomic groups.

The historian Romila Thapar sees the beginnings of an unhealthy dogmatism, an attribute Hinduism has been largely spared in the past. Several years before a mob of militant Hindus stormed and demolished the Babri Masjid in Ayodhya to make way for a temple at what they insist was the birthplace of the god-king Rama (thus the temple's name, the Ram Janmabhoomi), she warned that discussion of the mosque-temple issue was being cut off by zealots who were being cheered by the middle class. She criticized the national television network, then under the control of Prime Minister Rajiv Gandhi's government, for fueling this militancy by showing a strictly sectarian, northern Hindu version of the *Ramayana* in the long-running serialization of the epic. At about the same time, militant Hindus were making holy bricks in public ceremonies in many states, preparing the building blocks of their controversial temple in Ayodhya, whose cornerstone Gandhi ultimately permitted them to erect, against the better judgment of some within his own party. It was a time of rising religious passion. "There was no attempt made to try to suggest to viewers that there are other versions of the *Ramayana*, that the story was not in origin a religious text, but was converted into a religious text at a certain point in time historically," Thapar said. "Instead, the story was projected simply as a major belief of the majority community. There was absolutely no discussion."

"If you have to have a national culture, what do you do?" asked Thapar, professor of ancient history at Jawaharlal Nehru University. (Her late brother and sister-in-law, Romesh and Raj Thapar, founded India's most penetrating intellectual journal, *Seminar*.) "You pick up the cultural idioms of the majority and you project those as the national culture. If you had watched Indian television over the last ten years, you would imagine that there really wasn't anybody else except a whole bunch of upper caste Hindus that constituted Indian society. There was very little reflection of other religious groups or for that matter of the problems that are facing the lower castes and dalits today." Dalits, "the oppressed," like harijans, "the children of god," are two other terms for untouchables, the first a self-chosen name, the second bestowed on them by Mahatma Gandhi.

"This projection of national culture has been a bonanza for the middle class, and the media picked that up," Thapar said. "The whole dialogue about national culture is now going on within the Hindu middle class, and when you see that the middle class is such a small percentage of the totality of Indian humanity it seems so unfair that the views and perceptions of other people are not entering into the debate at all. Now you cannot talk about the Ayodhya problem. You cannot discuss the Babri Masjid–Ram Janmabhoomi because it has become a matter of belief. People say, well, a miracle was performed, and idols to Rama were found in the mosque in 1949. You can't begin to say, who put those idols there? Why did the god Rama choose 1949 as the year to reveal his birthplace? This kind of dogmatic position is frightening because it means that even on the broader issues, discussions of Indian civilization, or what constitutes Indian society, debate gets completely closed down. Either you agree with this view or else you're anti-Indian."

More positively, the same middle classes are producing other kinds of activists whose energies are going into more secular causes like consumer protection, the environment, and urban conservation. Some are creating un-official civic institutions, citizens' groups beyond the reach of the politicians who have come to dominate too many aspects of Indian life. Though these activists are a very small minority representing disparate causes, rarely able to communicate effectively with each other, they sense that new ways must be found to hold bureaucrats and politicians accountable, since many voters believe that the ballot alone has not given them the control they should have over their elected representatives. Development cannot be left in the hands of government alone, they say.

H. D. Shourie, the founder of the consumer organization Common Cause, was one the earliest leaders of the campaign for greater citizens' rights. Common Cause, named for the American organization that inspired it, has gradually developed into a lobby group trying to force the central and state governments to implement a 1986 Consumer Protection Act that is being widely disregarded. Shourie, a former magistrate and director-general of the Indian Institute of Foreign Trade, has more or less led a single-handed battle to make government services and nationalized industries beholden to consumers through the law.

"The public sector must start realizing that they can't take the people for granted," Shourie said in a conversation in his New Delhi home, where the phone never stopped ringing and visitors dropped in unannounced. He has taken on the domestic national air carrier, Indian Airlines, the public service utilities, government pension plans that inexplicably withhold payments, and other agencies bogged down in what he calls "apathy and red-tapism." Common Cause doesn't take up individual complaints, but deals with broader policy problems and class-action suits, Shourie explained, adding that local consumer groups and newly established tribunals (where they are functioning) should deal with specific cases. I went to watch one of these tribunals in action. On that day there were a number of complaints against service shops and retailers who refused to honor warranties.

Meaningless guarantees, false advertising, and the widespread marketing of fake merchandise, sometimes with lethal consequences, are problems every Indian consumer meets with depressing regularity. Cosmetics and perfumes, foods, edible oils, and a range of drinks are adulterated or concocted to be sold under pirated brand names, domestic and foreign. Watches, clothing, and shoes and luxuries like sunglasses are faked. Kerosene is sometimes mixed with diesel fuel; gasoline is watered down. Hundreds die each year from lethal products, some of which are intended for children. In January 1991, a color supplement of the Calcutta newspaper, *The Telegraph*, described in an investigative report how baby formula was adulterated: "Analysts have found that adulterers of milk powder first buy tins of genuine baby food. Then they carefully cut out the tinfoil and replace half the product with an inferior quality of talcum powder, wheat or rice dust. The tinfoil is carefully sealed again and the product sold to shopkeepers at a lower price. On consumption, these may lead to death or permanent disability." The reporters also found cat and rat flesh sold as unspecified "meat" to restaurants, red-painted apples, and phony soft drinks in original bottles with their old lids hammered back on. It is a commonly held assumption that bottles of "foreign" whiskeys and brandies (always bootlegged, since they cannot be freely imported) are almost inevitably adulterated or diluted. It is probably not apocryphal that more Johnny Walker Black Label "scotch" is reported to be sold in India alone each year than the company manufactures. Copyright and patent protection is a major issue of contention in trade talks between India and Europe or the United States. Brazenly, a town on India's west coast called Usa does a brisk business labeling fakes "Made in USA." An Indian tourist interviewed on a buying spree in Singapore by the magazine *India Today* said the obvious. The best thing about shopping in Singapore beside reasonable prices, he observed, was that "all the items are genuine."

Consumer groups all over India struggle against almost impossible odds to make the products people buy safer. There are few if any independent testing laboratories, and government authorities asked to examine suspect goods frequently accept bribes to switch samples or give fraudulent clearances, with no regard to the dangers to public health. Hundreds of people die annually of unsafe medicines or are contaminated in dirty hospitals. In New Delhi, a medical supplier, S. K. Kataria, fought for more than two years to bring charges against a manufacturer of intravenous drips who supplied him with bottles of tainted dextrose and saline solutions. Some of the bottles he showed me in his warehouse had visible fungus growths. Kataria, backed by Shourie's Common Cause, was able to convince the Central Bureau of Investigation, India's FBI, to enter the case when he found proof that clear samples had been substituted for bottles sent for testing on the way to the lab. Several drug enforcement officials were charged. Meanwhile, reports of tainted blood supplies—some with the acquired immune deficiency syndrome virus—were beginning to circulate. With an AIDS epidemic now taking shape in India, a specialist in Bombay told me, blood transfusions will be a major transmitter, along with unsafe sex. A majority of hospitals and blood banks do not routinely test for the virus.

While adulteration and fakery may never be curbed, Shourie and Common Cause did score a landmark victory in getting authorities to change the practice of allowing packaged consumer goods to be sold with the wording "local taxes extra." "That 'local taxes extra' imprinted along with suggested retail prices on packages creates enormous problems for consumers," Shourie said. "Stores are supposed to display what these taxes are, because they are not standardized nationally, but I would say that not one shop in the country does. In 99.9 percent of the cases, there is no receipt given that shows what taxes are paid. So merchants have been fleecing the people in collusion with the politicians. More than $2 billion is going into the pockets of shopkeepers and the politicians every year. Retail stores were simply charging whatever they could get away with. Or the correct taxes were collected but never paid to the government."

A neglected environment severely pressed by galloping population growth and unregulated industries is another cause drawing Indians into action groups. The fragmentary information they are beginning to collect is staggering in its implications. Mahesh Chander Mehta, a lawyer willing to take on environmental class action suits, told a newspaper that illegal stone crushing around New Delhi sends 1,500 tons of dust into the air daily, contributing to the capital's rapid rise into the World Health Organization's list of the earth's most polluted cities. Mehta said that when a court mandated a medical study in 1985, a team of court-appointed doctors found that 70 percent of the first 1,500 people examined around the stone quarries had tuberculosis. In the industrial zone of Patancheru, near the southern city of Hyderabad, Dr. Krishna Rao has catalogued 2,000 acres of fertile land destroyed by chemical pollutants that poisoned wells up to 145 feet deep. More than three hundred factories operate in Patancheru, all of them in theory subject to environmental laws. But lax regulators, corrupt politicians, and malleable judges friendly to industry have allowed many to flout restrictions. Rao points out metal bridges corroded by chemically polluted streams, children suffering from oxygen deficiencies and chemical burns, and one neighboring hamlet where no baby has been born alive for two years.

Mohan Dharia, the maverick who ran the national Planning Commission under the maverick Prime Minister Chandra Shekhar, says that more half of the land of India is in degraded condition. Dharia, a veteran environmentalist and founder of Vanarai, the People's Movement to Green India, has been observing the destruction of forests for several decades. He and most experts agree that there is no more than about 10 percent forest cover in India now, and that is rapidly depleting. At independence in 1947, between 20 and 30 percent of India was wooded. "By the early '80s," Dharia says, yearly demand on wood was about 133 million tons, while the supply was 39 million tons. By 2000 the total shortage will be 190 million tons, a third of that needed for fuel and industrial use."

Dharia has consistently scorned government promises to reforest India, particularly a 1985 plan that confidently promised a forest cover of 30 percent by the end of this century. Then on the political sidelines, Dharia (who had served Indira Gandhi as a minister before going over to the opposition) made a few calculations. Noting that the Seventh National Plan talked grandly of nurseries that would raise 800 million plants to supply a vast people's environment army, Dharia observed that a year later, in 1986, there were no plants to be seen. Indeed, no one had bothered to identify the five million hectares that was to be set aside each year for new growth. Dharia calculated that to meet the goals of 30 percent forest cover by the turn of the century, foresters would have to plant up to 20 trillion trees a year. India is a big country. The project hasn't been heard from since.

Dharia is among those environmentalists who believe that Indians must make tough decisions without delay if any forest cover is to be saved. Seventy percent of wood cut is being used for cooking, he said, a waste that cannot continue. In some cities, efforts are being made to build electric crematoriums since Hindus, who traditionally cremate their dead, have been using huge quantities of timber for funeral pyres. The change will be slow, however; several religious leaders in the holy city of Varanasi are protesting.

Farm animals and wandering herds that pillage the undergrowth, strip saplings, and destroy fragile grasses before they can sink roots will have to be removed from protected forests, most experts say. Ashok Khosla, head of Development Alternatives—an independent research institution that sees itself as a franchiser of simple, cheap, and environmentally sound implements for home and farmland—experimented with land reclamation in Madhya Pradesh. Khosla says that barren land regarded as lost to desertification can become productive in only a few seasons if rainwater is trapped in ponds and the land fenced off from grazing animals. Chandra Shekhar, the former prime minister, discovered the same thing at his small country retreat in the stony hills of Gurgaon, not far from New Delhi. Villagers there had told him nothing would grow because the land had been dead for centuries. He proved them wrong in five years. Around his large rainwater pond, he now grows grass, flowers, and fruit trees.

"It is time to announce that the holy cows, and other animals having no use, cannot be allowed to graze freely at the cost of society," Dharia wrote in 1987, but without much hope. Environmental conservation groups know that it would be impossible and unacceptable to force changes in traditional habits when there are no practical alternatives to cooking fires, hearths for heating, common land for grazing, and the slash-and-burn agriculture still widely practiced in remote areas. India might have been able to sustain and nurture these traditional styles of living, but only if there had been the political will to curb population and protect the environment decades ago. Because too much time has been lost, the options now are increasingly narrowed.

Environmentalists despair of changing persistent government preferences for gigantic projects like large irrigation dams that uproot millions of already disadvantaged people (and are rarely maintained adequately after construction). They argue fruitlessly for investment in many more small-scale developments that would bring quicker returns. But as Maneka Gandhi, a former minister of state for the environment, pointed out, there are no fortunes to be made in commissions on small projects. Environmentalists know that they are no match for the business and political interests who profit from large projects, particularly construction contractors and logging companies. Since independence, says Dharia, who was part of Mahatma Gandhi's Freedom Movement, "the unholy alliance of forest officers, politicians and contractors have taken a heavy toll." The outlook for India's environment is very grim.

At grassroots level, however, Indian activists in many fields including environmental protection are learning to plug into international networks for help and advice, overcoming the country's severe communications handicaps and official reluctance to internationalize problems and thereby damage the country's image. Many youthful Indians, educated in the United States, bring back new concepts of "single-issue" politics free of the ideological constructs that hobbled earlier generations of intellectuals who saw all problems in East-West or North-South terms, and failed to notice (or refused to admit) that the most powerful and effective movements for the environment, human rights, and feminism were growing in the industrialized nations.

A common language helps. Many young middle class Indians, more mobile than their parents or grandparents and therefore more likely to cross linguistic lines even if they never leave India, are communicating with each other and the outside world in English, to the consternation of North India's linguistic nationalists, who dream of making Hindi the dominant national language. The novelist Shashi Tharoor says that he is a good example of the English-speaking generation. He was born in London of Malayalam-speaking parents from South India and educated in Calcutta, where Bengali is spoken, and New Delhi, in the Hindi belt. He stoutly defends the use of English and Indians who use it. Writing without affectations and inhibitions, and with a perfect grasp of English idiom, he and other authors are opening worlds previously closed by language barriers, to the benefit of both foreigners and other Indians. There are dozens of books by such authors, with new titles appearing every year. The little universe of an iconoclastic minor civil servant, for example, is the subject of *English, August: An Indian Story*, by Upamayu Chatterjee. The breezily trashy social life of India's cinema capital, Bombay—Bollywood to those who love it—is superbly and wittily exposed in the honest books of a new novelist and former gossip columnist Shobha De, author of *Socialite Evenings* and *Starry Nights*.

"The Indian novel in English is as legitimate as the Indian novel in any Indian language, because the novel form itself was an import," Tharoor said over lunch in Delhi as he talked about *The Great Indian Novel*, his political satire based on the *Mahabharata*. "In my case, because I grew up in Bombay, Calcutta, and Delhi, the only language I had in common with my school-mates in all these places was English. The only language I have in common with my wife is English. She's half Kashmiri, half Bengali. My family's from Kerala. Our languages are as far apart as English and Russian. So the common language of people like us is very much our natural language of expression. But we use that language to express ideas and issues and stories that matter to us as Indians. This novel of mine is a novel that has been written in English but it is simultaneously a novel that could only have been written by an Indian."

Back in Bangalore, Vikram and Smita, also with diverse family roots, inhabit a similar linguistic world. Their son, Siddharth, whose first words were spoken in English, goes to an English-language nursery school and will be enrolled in English-medium private primary and secondary schools after that. In Srinagar, Kashmiri guerrilla leaders speak to reporters in English; in the back alleys of Patna, Biharis of the neo-leftist Indian People's Front, formed to battle for the civil rights of the undercastes, gave their organization an English-language name. And so it goes from town to town and city to city. In Delhi the writer Khushwant Singh, who calls English his mother tongue, is relieved to know that the use of the language is surviving the Indianization of India—and that the two are not incompatible.

"Most of us of the old generation really felt that English was a dying language here and that there would not be much coming out in the way of creative fiction," he said, soon after the publication of his latest work, a phantasmagorical history of his home city called simply *Delhi*. "But just the reverse has happened. A larger and larger number of young Indians have been turning out better novels in English than anything that my generation was able to do." There is another difference, said Singh, reflecting on the new urban, English-speaking Indian middle class and how it thinks and writes. "We were anglicized," he said. "These people are internationalized."

III

INDIA AND THE WORLD

9

A Subcontinent Adrift

Nations of a continental size, where much of life goes on in small villages and towns deep in the interior, away from the crosscurrents of international thought and commerce, are often prone to isolationism. "Large countries are very self-oriented in many ways," says Giri Deshingkar, one of a small corps of Indian experts on China, with which he draws some comparisons where foreign affairs are concerned. The American people, far richer and more literate than Indians, are certainly not renowned for the depth of their knowledge in geography and foreign affairs, and the United States, despite all its advanced communications technology, its immigrants, and its world role, has never been immune to isolationism. Indeed, fears of America turning inward are stronger in the post–Cold War era than they have been in nearly a century. In India, the new age poses even more complex and fundamental problems. If the United States has lost the galvanizing threat of an all-purpose enemy in the collapse of the Soviet Union, India has lost the very legs on which its foreign policy stood. A long and friendly relationship with Moscow, India's diplomatic protector abroad and often its mentor at home, is in shambles. New Delhi's cherished platform of nonalignment is without relevance in a world no longer polarized but sinking into dangerous nationalisms and regional strife. Official India's attitudes toward foreigners—symbolized by frequent noncooperation with international organizations, repeated refusals to join nuclear nonproliferation regimes, and the powerful undercover role ceded to intelligence agencies in foreign affairs—were rooted in long years of association with the former Soviet bloc and in a narrow (and always convenient) reading of regional history, which assigned this nation an unmistakably imperial role in South Asia. If India is to integrate better with its neighbors and with the larger industrial world, as it must for its economic future, decades of lessons absorbed by new entrants to the Indian Foreign Service will have to be unlearned. In short, India moves toward the twenty-first century in need of new foreign policies and a new generation of experts—perhaps drawn from Khushwant Singh's "internationalized" youthful middle class—to apply these policies skillfully in a transformed international atmosphere. New policies call for profound changes in Indian thinking, not just hasty and superficial gestures of goodwill toward nations once regularly and safely reviled by the Indian establishment. These sudden overtures from former critics don't fool foreigners, long accustomed to wandering on the fringes of diplomatic Delhi, always suspect and therefore frozen out of serious debate, learning on the sidelines what a recent American ambassador, William Clark, Jr., called the "virtue of patience." Indian isolationism is often rooted less in popular indifference or the political necessity of putting domestic policies first and more in an unexamined arrogance and sense of self-sufficiency.

"Foreigners are irrelevant to Indian politics," John Gunther Dean, one of Washington's most experienced diplomats, said not long before he completed his term as ambassador in New Delhi four years before Clark's tenure ended. "India is wrapped up in India." India has trouble with the outside world on many levels. Those humorless officers at passport control are not an immigration service but the local police. They are symbols of an unsympathetic system that scares away tourists and leaves foreigners begging for decades for the right to apply for citizenship or live in India without it, always just a step ahead of deportation. Foreign, especially Western, scholars are discouraged as much as possible from moving around India to do extensive research or from working in many Indian institutions. All donations from abroad, even from one private foundation to an Indian counterpart, are expected to pass through official channels. One example: A small grant from Canada a few years ago for a struggling schizophrenia center in Madras, the first clinic of its kind in India, had to clear seven government ministries and was tied up for months in the scrutiny process. And if New Delhi, a national capital city of about nine million people, has a less than cosmopolitan air, blame the absence of true ethnic neighborhoods and little restaurants with international cuisines, along with the paucity of foreign films, music, and art from other Asian nations and the Pacific as well as from Africa, Latin America, Europe, and the United States. Officially, immigrants are not welcome, and so no footloose Corsican or Greek or Peace Corps dropout stays behind to start a cafe. The Peace Corps was in fact ordered out of India by Indira Gandhi, wary as always that it could function as a vehicle for American intelligence. Students from friendly Third World nations say that they are often lonely in a society where dating is confined to the avant-garde, and that they are sometimes harassed by landlords and made to feel socially unacceptable because of their nationality or race. To avoid AIDS, says the Indian Council for Medical Research, adhere to Indian culture and don't have sex with foreigners. Never mind that most hospitals don't test blood and that organ transplants or other operations may be performed in less-than-sterile environments.

When Indians move abroad—they are called, significantly, Nonresident Indians, shortened to NRIs by a nation with a mania for initials—the Indian government encourages them to give their first allegiance and highest priority (financially as well as emotionally) to the land of their birth. Publications in Delhi and Bombay regularly quote parents settled in the United States who cling to Indian neighborhoods in the hope of shutting out the new world, determined to block the "Americanization" of their children, who sooner or later are apt to feel the tension. Emigrants like these—though certainly not all Indians who live abroad—seem to see nothing questionable about extracting professional satisfaction and large incomes from a nation to which they choose not to make a personal commitment. When Indian children do well in Western schools, which they almost always do, it is their Indianness that is praised in the Indian media, not the opportunities given to them by their adopted countries. Paradoxically, when NRIs heed the call to come home and invest their substantial talents in India, they can find themselves treated as semi-traitors with Western ideas who no longer fit in. The pattern is uneven, as always in India. Conversations with NRIs in New Delhi and Bombay indicate that people in private business or branches of international corporations usually have an easier transition because a more cosmopolitan atmosphere prevails. Scientists in government service and scholars in state-run universities often have a harder time.

A lot of this anti-foreign ethos has been fostered by official India or, to a decreasing extent, intellectual India, and it runs counter to the innate generosity of the Indian people, at home or abroad. When political commentators in New Delhi were aghast that the Congress Party's first candidate to replace the slain Rajiv Gandhi as party leader was his Italian-born widow, Sonia, villagers in the agricultural state of Haryana told me that her foreignness did not bother them. In their view, she merely came from another place—they used the word *desh* (state or nation) interchangeably to mean another country, another Indian state, or just "somewhere else." Sonia Gandhi had made her home in India, they told me, and that made her Indian, just as a Rajasthani girl who marries a Haryanvi becomes a Haryanvi. This natural tendency to incorporate most (though not all) outsiders seems to exist everywhere except in the offices of government, the armed forces, and in certain concentrations of scholars and social activists who take a particularly hostile view of the industrialized world, which they blame for many of India's developmental problems. When a Navy officer in civilian clothes, driving too fast and close in his Maruti, hit our car in Delhi traffic, he said he could not discuss the damage with us because military men were not allowed to talk to foreigners. Wrapped in the immunity of the flag, he drove away.

Indians are raised on two unquestioned truths: that Indian (or Hindu) civilization is superior to most (probably all) others, and that any foreign power that begins to take on imperial shape will sooner or later threaten India. To the latter we might add a corollary: that most (if not all) of India's problems are caused by somebody else. Throughout its pre-1947 history, the Subcontinent—particularly what is now North India and the northern tier of Pakistan on the vast Indo-Gangetic plain—suffered invasions and conquests. For Hindus, the history of Hindustan began with migrations in about 1500 B.C. of Indo-European people who upper-caste Hindus claim were their light-skinned Aryan ancestors. Anthropologists and historians reject this attempt to define Aryans in ethnic or racial terms; it is a resilient myth, however, provoking continuing controversy in India. In the millennia that followed, Persian, Hellenistic, Turkish, Afghan, Mughal, and British conquerors, exploiters, and colonizers came by land and then sea. Before the curtain came down on colonialism, the Portuguese and French had also snatched territory on India's coasts. The Japanese got to the portals of Northeast India in World War II. China's Communist regime, consolidating territory after overrunning Tibet, struck independent India in 1962. Pakistan tried to take Indian Kashmir at least twice.

The colonial experience seems to have traumatized Indians and continues to obsess them with an immediacy no longer found in Malaysia or Singapore, also ex-colonies of the British, or in Indonesia, where the Dutch had a far worse record in dealing with local people. The Netherlands left Indonesia with almost no development, least of all in human resources. When the British withdrew from India, the new nation inherited good roads, railways, schools, hospitals, hotels (and resthouses in unlikely places), libraries, museums, and the most magnificently planned capital city in Asia. Foreigners are not alone in sensing an extreme sensitivity in mainstream India to any but the most negative references to the colonial era. When a Sikh political leader was searching for an exceptionally nasty insult to indicate his contempt for the establishment, he lowered his voice to a conspiratorial pitch and growled: "Who are these Hindus anyway? For 800 years they cleaned the utensils of the Moslems and the British."

A strong Hindu Indian sense of cultural superiority has contributed to a surprising lack of interest in and, indeed, condemnation of the nearby nations of Southeast Asia—particularly Thailand, Malaysia, and Indonesia— whose development has well outstripped India's, leaving the Subcontinent a generation behind by most measures. When I moved to Delhi after four years in Bangkok, a lot of people, including government officials, took the opportunity to remark how unfortunate it was that Southeast Asians had lost their cultural roots in the rush to materialism, assuming that I would bolster their prejudices with my own experience. The contention would be hotly disputed by Thais and even more certainly by Indonesians, most of whom believe they can balance quick economic growth and a sharply reduced population increase with their artistic and spiritual heritage. They would argue that Buddhism and Islam have been more egalitarian in outlook and responsive to the needs of all sectors of society than Hinduism. When the then–Indian prime minister, V. P. Singh, went to Malaysia for a meeting of leaders of developing nations in 1990, Indian reporters who accompanied him were astounded at the splendor of Kuala Lumpur, with its wide, clean boulevards, new office towers, restored old city neighborhoods, and lack of slums. The quality of life is unquestionably better for most people in Southeast Asia, excluding Indochina, as impartial United Nations and World Bank indicators demonstrate. India's great advantages over Thais, Malaysians, or Indonesians were the political and intellectual freedom all Indians enjoyed, but these are now being eroded by an increasingly unresponsive, undemocratic, self-serving political system that is also not meeting social needs. As for Burma, there lurks in the hearts of many Indians the conviction that it should be part of India, or at least a Greater India, *Maha Bharat*, stretching from Afghanistan to some hazy Indochinese horizon. The Burmese, were they given a chance, would more likely express a kinship with Southeast Asia or China instead. As a result, New Delhi's foreign policy establishment watches Burma very closely.

The historian Romila Thapar says that disdain or indifference toward other Asian nations stems in part from the traditional education of Indians. "There is a tendency to see everything in terms of what we were brought up to look for: the Indian influence on . . . whatever part of the world it may be. The notion that in fact there was interaction with other cultures, other civilizations; that there were whole areas where techniques and ideas came from somewhere else, the notion of the need for intermeshing in order to understand a culture—that was all absent. The world around was seen in terms of, did India influence another culture or not? If it didn't, then there really wasn't too much interest in learning about it. Southeast Asia, for example, was talked of as part of a Greater India, and there was a terribly condescending attitude toward Southeast Asians. A whole series of historians from the 1930s to the 1950s projected this notion that Southeast Asia was an extension of Indian culture. But for Indian civilization, they said, there would be very little to see or do there. This is being very dramatically corrected now, with excavations and historical work being done in Southeast Asia. But the attitude weighs on us."

Thapar, an internationally known author and professor of ancient Indian history at Jawaharlal Nehru University, is fascinated by the changes that have taken place in transplanted Indian culture over the centuries since Hindu kings ruled distant areas from Indochina to Indonesia. "Take the *Ramayana*," she said, in a conversation in her quiet home filled with art and books. "People keep talking about how the *Ramayana* is found all over and that this is part of a lingering Hindu presence in Southeast Asia. The interesting thing about the *Ramayana* is that there are multiple versions, and practically any group of any cultural importance has its own version. This is the case even in India. What is interesting for the historian is to do a comparative study of these diversities and see what they are telling us, because they are telling us something. They are telling us about dialogues that once went on, that focused on the story but said much more. You have, for example, the Indonesian *Ramayanas*, which are hardly even the bare bones of the same story. They have incorporated a whole lot of Islamic belief and mythology."

Although Indians ventured abroad from earliest times, taking their civilization to Southeast Asia and the shores of Africa, India never became a great maritime nation. A religious prohibition eventually developed against crossing the "black waters" of the open seas, an act that could "pollute" an upper caste Hindu. Before Mohandas Karamchand Gandhi left for England as a student in the late nineteenth century, he was formally stripped of his Modh Bania subcaste by his kinsmen. He was also warned against the more practical contaminants of the West: meat-eating, alcohol, and easy women. Nearly a century later, a retired sea captain told me how in the 1960s his mother had prayed and fasted almost to the point of death for fear of his pollution by ocean voyages, life in foreign ports, and a marriage outside his caste. Fear of pollution by strangers, I have also been told, also stymied the growth of a restaurant culture in India. In Brahmin homes, foreigners may be served meals, politely and subtly, from separate food dishes.

Through no fault of their own, Indians who do not travel or communicate frequently with relatives abroad have scant information at their disposal with which to judge the outside world. A lot of what they do hear about other nations reflects opinions planted in the media by the Ministry of External Affairs or Information and Broadcasting officials who control television and radio news. Most Indian newspapers and magazines do not have foreign correspondents permanently based abroad. A few have contributors who seem to confine themselves to rewriting publications in London and Washington; others rely on (but do not use extensively) the reports of the privately owned India Abroad News Service, based in New York and heavily weighted toward news from North America and Europe of special interest to Indians. International news agencies are filtered through two national networks, the Press Trust of India and United News of India. The PTI in particular is not averse to taking patriotic views of issues when foreign criticism of India is involved. In March 1991, when India faced tough questioning at the annual meeting of the United Nations Human Rights Commission in Geneva, the *National Herald*, the Congress Party–Nehru dynasty newspaper, used a PTI report that began with the assertion that New Delhi "came in for praise" for its human rights record, and then went on to record lengthily the speech of the then–Indian attorney general, G. Ramaswamy, which ducked every major point of contention and covered up documented infractions with misleading (and occasionally plainly dishonest) assurances of due process. In *The Hindustan Times*, the same PTI report had been merged with one from the India Abroad News Service, telling a different story. The lead in *The Hindustan Times* said that India had been confronted with grave accusations and had been asked to review its anti-terrorism laws. The article then quoted members of the Commission charging that these laws gave Indian security forces wide powers to kill without accountability, and were in violation of international covenants. Side by side, the two reports could have come from different meetings.

Both the PTI and UNI relay very little of what they receive from international news services to Indian and India-based foreign clients, who are by law not allowed to take reports directly from the big foreign agencies: the Associated Press, Reuters, or Agence France-Presse. This amounts to an extraordinary bar to the flow of information in a democracy, but one that will soon become meaningless as news organizations tap directly into international computer networks through telephone modems. Even on Delhi's bad telephone lines I could, if I persevered, connect to New York with a small laptop computer and call up international news agency reports of major stories. This was especially important for following events in Pakistan, where Indian news agencies could not be trusted to be objective or comprehensive in their reporting. When there is no direct electronic access to international news reports, Indians and foreigners alike rely on radio bulletins from the British Broadcasting Corporation or the Voice of America. More recently, Indians have begun turning to CNN International or a new BBC Asian television news service received through satellite dishes whose proliferation the government has tried but failed to control. The most famous and trusted foreigner in India over many years has probably been Mark Tully, the BBC's veteran South Asia correspondent, who grew up in India and speaks several of its languages. At a huge meeting of local people protesting a proposed dam to be built in the remote Narmada Valley of Madhya Pradesh, I could hear the word "marktully" pop up in village conversations. Demonstrators had been assured that the BBC was coming, and folks were checking all foreigners arriving at the dusty, sun-scorched site near the hamlet of Harsud to see if the great man might be among them.

Reports from agencies with a special interest in the developing world, such as Gemini in London and the Inter Press Service in Rome, are used only sporadically by the Indian press, as are other sources of news from the Third World, whose people and societies get almost no coverage in India despite New Delhi's claim to the leadership of the developing nations. Indians complain nonetheless that their view of the world is colored by Western domination of the media, an accusation that reached a hysterical pitch during the 1991 Persian Gulf war. Indians eager to stay abreast of events then flocked to the few hotels or homes with access to Cable News Network transmissions. Critics charged that viewers were being fed disinformation by CNN about war operations and casualties. Some Indians persist in believing, for example, that thousands of Americans were killed by the Iraqis during Operation Desert Storm, but that Washington was able to withhold this news from the media and people of the United States. (The Pentagon's death toll is 290, with only 148 of them combat casualties.) Indians had themselves to blame for the popularity of CNN during the brief war. Doordarshan, the government-run television monopoly, had no independent film footage from the Persian Gulf, and only one correspondent in the area, who telephoned audio reports from the safety of Bahrain or Dubai, well away from the battle zone. Around midnight on a tragic day a few months later, the network shut down inexplicably at its normal time just as reports began to come in of the assassination of Rajiv Gandhi. Many Indians turned once again to CNN, this time for important and devastating news about their own country.

With the exception of a few newspapers—most notably *The Times of India*, whose energetic foreign editor, Ramesh Chandran, dashed off to Baghdad, from which he was expelled with other foreign reporters, and then Amman, where he was marooned by Saudi Arabia's refusal to give him a visa, despite the requests of sympathetic American diplomats—the Indian press did not do much better than television in covering the Persian Gulf War. Editors who would like to expand coverage of foreign news say that cost alone cannot be used as an excuse for the refusal to open overseas bureaus or send reporters to important stories abroad, because in many cases the money is available. The problem, journalists say, is that wealthy proprietors of Indian publications often run them primarily as profit-making businesses or platforms for political influence, and refuse to spend money on international news, which is extremely expensive to gather independently. Government currency regulations also get in the way of wider news coverage. When distinguished Indian writers are sent abroad on assignment— journalists of the stature of the independent columnist S. Nihal Singh, *India Today's* Shekhar Gupta, or Nikhil Chakravartty, editor of the journal *Mainstream*—they are hobbled by limitations on the amount of foreign currency they may take and by a bar against Indians holding internationally accepted credit cards. S. Nihal Singh says that when he was forced to leave Baghdad by the Iraqis at the outbreak of war, he had to hitch a ride to Jordan with CBS News. In Iraq, his international telegraph and Telex card had been rejected by officials who wanted dollars or the American Express card in payment when he tried to send out reports. He had been allowed to take exactly $100 in American currency out of India, plus travelers' checks that the Iraqis would also not honor. India and Iraq had a close relationship at the time.

China is India's biggest neighbor and a persistent concern of policymakers. Yet Indians read or see virtually nothing about China and the Chinese in the media. India's own Chinese minority dwindled rapidly after a brief 1962 border war, when many Chinese-Indians decided to emigrate rather than face perennial distrust and sometimes open hostility, and most of their ethnic neighborhoods gradually disintegrated. Indians have scant knowledge of what China, which chose the path of totalitarian Communism when India opted for democracy, has made of itself, good or bad. When the confrontation between Chinese students and their government turned Beijing's Tiananmen Square into a battleground in 1989, no Indian publication except the innovative magazine *India Today* sent a reporter until the crisis was over. Giri Deshingkar, the China scholar at Delhi's Center for the Study of Developing Societies, said at the time that the one reporter on the scene, a correspondent for the Press Trust of India, was not an expert and could contribute little to Indian understanding of what was happening.

After tanks crushed the Tiananmen Square rebellion, Doordarshan, the Indian national television network, showed a brief segment of Chinese government news footage and reported that about twenty-three people had died, "most of them soldiers." India never condemned the attack on democracy. "The Indian government doesn't want to say anything that could be misinterpreted in Beijing or could cause the Chinese to start talking about Kashmir," Deshingkar said. John Lall, a diplomatic historian of the India-China border conflict, accused the Indian media of "parrotlike" repetition of the official Chinese line on Tiananmen Square. "I find it very sad that we don't have independent reporting from trouble spots," he said. "I wish someone in India would take steps to better inform the people."

The Indian media learned little from its dismal performance of reporting on Tiananmen Square. Television continued its ill-informed, unimaginative, and faint-hearted performance through the momentous months to come, offering perfunctory news bulletins and almost never calling on the considerable expertise of India's international scholars, columnists, or diplomats for commentary or documentary work. Before the year was out, Doordarshan had bungled the destruction of the Berlin Wall and the fall of Nicolae Ceaucescu in Romania, and then headed into 1990 unprepared for the general rout of East European Communism and the reunification of Germany. A year later, the attempted August coup against President Mikhail Gorbachev was getting second or third billing in the evening news within twenty-four hours, while the Soviet crisis remained unresolved. But by then, Indian diplomacy was also in confusion, and maybe it was deemed better to back off.

When the first reports of the coup reached India, Prime Minister P. V. Narasimha Rao greeted the premature announcement that Gorbachev had been overthrown with some tut-tutting over what happens to people who try to push reforms too fast and far. He also insisted that this was an internal affair of the Soviet Union, not a clarion call to democratic forces. Two days later, the Indian establishment was scrambling for some way to recover face when the coup collapsed and cranes moved in to lift images of Communist heroes off their pedestals in Moscow. As Shekhar Gupta pointed out in *India Today*, it was soon discovered that New Delhi, which was dependent on Moscow for defense supplies and a large amount of trade, had never bothered to get to know Boris Yeltsin. "Practically all the coup leaders were soft on India, but a new cabinet may be less considerate," Gupta wrote from the Russian capital. "Ignoring Yeltsin all these years might now prove to be costly for Indian policymakers."

Official India never saw incongruity in proclaiming itself the world's largest democracy (or the leader of the "nonaligned" world) while stubbornly believing that the Soviet Union was its firmest and most reliable friend, and often a country worth emulating. Weeks before the shattering events of August 1991 in Russia—amid a general assault on Communism, the liberation of the Baltic States, the renaming of Leningrad as St. Petersburg, and the rumbles of dissent throughout the outlying republics—India confidently renewed a twenty-year treaty of friendship and cooperation with Moscow, a relationship no other democratic nation had forged with the Kremlin. The original treaty had been signed by Indira Gandhi just before the Bangladesh war in 1971 without parliamentary or public debate—the country learned about it after the fact—but the accord was never seriously challenged by any segment of the Indian political spectrum. Nor was there any effective opposition to its renewal. There was an unexamined, almost childlike quality to India's loyalty to Moscow, and one is tempted to make a leap into Indian psycho-political analysis to begin to explain this diplomatic phenomenon.

In *The Inner World*, his examination of the Hindu mind, the psychoanalyst Sudhir Kakar makes the observation that the Indian emerges from childhood convinced that he is lovable and expecting to be universally loved. He (perhaps more than she) is also prepared to give his all to an authority figure, but always assumes that there will be benefits in return. Moscow, unconsciously or deliberately—perhaps papers still to be disgorged from the Kremlin will tell—was able to manipulate India's upper-caste Hindu establishment very skillfully by doling out just the right amount of material and psychological payback on India's emotional investment in the relationship. India served Soviet interests in that vast area of territory between Central Asia and the Indian Ocean, blowing the whistle at every Chinese or American move in the region and acting as a funnel for Soviet propaganda and a reliable place to plant untrue stories in the press. In turn, Moscow bought Indian commodities and second-rate consumer goods, kept the Kashmir issue out of the United Nations—where resolutions calling for a plebiscite have been pending since 1948—and generally protected India in international forums, contributing to Indian immunity from human rights scrutiny. Soviet leaders lavished attention on visiting Indians and fueled the inflated self-importance of Indira Gandhi and her son Rajiv in international affairs. In 1986, Gorbachev went to India and signed a joint statement calling for an end to nuclear weapons worldwide. It was christened the Delhi Declaration and Indians talked about it endlessly while the rest of the world took no notice. When it appeared that Rajiv Gandhi would be defeated in 1989, a Soviet diplomat took me to lunch in Delhi and wanted to know everything I could possibly tell him about Vishwanath Pratap Singh, who would soon become prime minister, and the rest of the Indian political opposition. "All this time we have known only one family," he said gloomily. "This was a mistake." He needn't have worried too much. Singh made a former ambassador to Moscow, Inder Kumar Gujral, his foreign minister, and the relationship survived longer than the Soviet Union.

The courting of India by Moscow and its former Soviet bloc clients embraced the Indian cultural establishment as well as the diplomatic corps. A generation of film critics, writers, performers, and artists were feted in Moscow, Warsaw, Prague, Budapest, and Bucharest. Astonishingly, many never saw the failures and unhappiness around them, even in the waning years of Communism. The journalist N. Ram, a leftist, admitted candidly in 1990 that many Indians were stunned by the depth of hatred for the system revealed by the people of one Eastern European nation after another as Communist regimes collapsed with breathtaking speed.

Ainslie Embree, the Columbia University scholar who lived in India for long periods and has been visiting the country regularly for more than four decades, sees a number of factors behind the willingness of Indian intellectuals to believe what they were told about the old Soviet bloc. "First of all, they didn't speak the language," he said. "There are virtually no Indians who can speak Russian, even people high up in the Indian Communist parties who went to Moscow and people who teach Russian studies in the universities. And then there is another side. You never would see in any Indian newspaper any discussion or denunciation of the lack of freedom in Russia. It was never, never mentioned. Whereas in the old days—and this is something that has now ceased in Indian newspapers—everybody always brought up the condition of American blacks. They don't do that so much now, maybe because of how they treat their own people." News about America was limited, he added, except for certain stories. The case of Julius and Ethel Rosenberg, who were executed for spying, was repeatedly mentioned. "The Rosenbergs were famous in India for a long time," he said.

"There was something else very complicated that was going on, and I can't document it," Embree said in a conversation in New York. "The Indians saw the Russians as Third World people who had made it. They could feel empathy with the Russians. They could also feel superior to the Russians. They dressed in funny clothes and their women weren't svelte."

Many diplomats and some Indian journalists believe that some newspapers and India's two news agencies had over the years been influenced and occasionally manipulated by Moscow or Indians working in the interests of the old Soviet Union. During the Cold War, the Bombay weekly *Blitz* and its editor R. K. Karanjia willingly printed scurrilous reports of American wrongdoing, usually spying or meddling in Indian domestic affairs, many of the accounts pure fabrications that caused grave problems for United States diplomats in the region. Though the world had changed and the Cold War had largely evaporated by 1991, *Blitz* was certain that the United States Central Intelligence Agency had been involved in the plot to kill Rajiv Gandhi. A report on June 8, 1991, was headlined "Gates of Hell," a reference to Robert Gates, who was then about to undergo confirmation hearings on his appointment as Director of Central Intelligence. During the Persian Gulf War, *Blitz* repeated the false assertions that the United States was bombing the sacred Muslim shrines at Najaf and Karbala in Iraq. Karanjia himself wrote: "And all this because President Bush has worked himself into the paranoid belief that Saddam Hussein is the Antichrist of the old Christian prophecies and had to be destroyed by any means, foul or fair." Karanjia, meanwhile, had been rewarded with a seat in India's upper house of Parliament, the Rajya Sabha, for his service to journalism, or possibly his usefulness to the Congress Party and its foreign friends.

A former reporter for the Press Trust of India told me of news releases from Soviet bloc nations (or the Indian Embassy in Moscow) going out on the wire without checking or rewriting. Sometimes, this reporter said, Indian intelligence officials were also involved in planting stories or using the news agency to gather information through correspondents in neighboring nations. Another former reporter filed a complaint with the watchdog Press Council when a Soviet-related story he did not write appeared under his name. The directors of the Press Trust of India deny accusations of pro-Soviet bias, but the charges are too frequent and widely circulated to be dismissed without further independent investigation, a job for a courageous Indian journalism school if not the Indian press.

A few Indians think that Soviet activity in India extended beyond the attempt to influence news. Rama Swarup, a businessman who tried to form an anti-Communist lobby in India to counter the influence on policy of the Soviet Union and the Indian left, believes that he was arrested on espionage charges in 1985 at the behest of the KGB. Swarup, a committed and outspoken enemy of the left, who had joined the World Anti-Communist League in Seoul in the early 1960s, was Taiwan's trade representative in India and an occasional consultant for other nations, including Israel, with which India, in deference to Arab states' wishes, then had only minimal diplomatic relations at consular level. He was accused of spying for Taiwan and Israel as well as the United States and what was then West Germany. Denied bail, he spent a year in a high-security prison and three and a half years in solitary confinement under house arrest in New Delhi before he was released by a judge who remarked that the Indian government seemed to be "looking for a black cat in a black room." Officials were never able to find grounds to prosecute him, but Swarup has feared since that they would try again. In addition to forming the first organized anti-Soviet lobby in India, he had been calling for an investigation into suspicions that Indira Gandhi had foreign bank accounts in contravention of Indian law. He was arrested under the Rajiv Gandhi administration, a regime that was soon to face charges that officials had been taking kickbacks from the Swedish arms manufacturer Bofors AG and other defense contractors. Swarup's case was reviewed and ultimately dropped more than four years later, in 1990, only because the Congress Party (and the Gandhi family) were then out of power.

Swarup is a controversial figure, partly a zealot and partly a gregarious, talkative man with many influential friends in India who defend his integrity even when they do not share his resolutely anti-Communist views. When I met him several months after his release, he had set up office in a barren rented house and was trying to rebuild a disrupted life and business. He was also resuming the collection of information on Soviet activities in India, most recently during the 1979–1989 war in Afghanistan. During that time, he said, the Soviet Embassy staff mushroomed in Delhi and KGB activity increased sharply. But he argues that this is not unusual. In every crisis involving Moscow in Asia, including Vietnam, where the level of direct Soviet involvement in the war against the United States is just beginning to be revealed, India was used as a diplomatic base, Swarup says. New Delhi supported Moscow's invasion of Afghanistan, and when anti-government Afghan refugees began turning up in India, officials tried to deny their existence, forcing representatives of the United Nations High Commissioner for Refugees to operate almost clandestinely in their efforts to interview them. Before each visit to Delhi of an important Kabul regime official, unfriendly Afghans were rounded up and imprisoned for a few days.

When Rajiv Gandhi, speaking with a few foreign correspondents he had invited to tea at his home, was asked to explain the rationale behind India's policy on Afghanistan, he said—off the record, though he was out of government—that it had been more or less foisted on his mother by her advisers when she needed a quick response to the Soviet invasion. More than a decade later, with Soviet troops gone from Afghanistan, India was still cheering whatever regime Moscow had most recently installed in Kabul, sometimes outdoing the Soviet Union in fervor. In 1990, President Najibullah was feted on a state visit to India at about the same time that Moscow had begun looking for ways to ease him out of office in Afghanistan. During the war, India's loyalty and assistance to Moscow and Kabul were a constant irritant to Pakistan, which, with the United States, Britain, Saudi Arabia, and others, backed the Afghan rebel armies. Many Pakistanis talked darkly of the ease with which India could open hostilities over divided Kashmir, or anywhere else along a dangerously vulnerable border, leaving Pakistan with a war on two fronts. The ultimate irony was that when Najibullah fell from power in April 1992, a few months after Boris Yeltsin's Russia withdrew military aid, India quickly backed off from an offer of exile to the Afghan leader.

On a visit to Bangkok in 1986, Rajiv Gandhi had indicated that New Delhi was operating with a pre-packaged policy on Cambodia, too. India was the only non-Communist nation that officially recognized the Phnom Penh regime of Heng Samrin and Hun Sen when it was installed by the Vietnamese Army after it overthrew Pol Pot in 1979. A majority of United Nations member states gave varying degrees of support to the coalition of resistance forces (including Pol Pot's) that held Cambodia's General Assembly seat. Heng Samrin and Hun Sen were former Khmer Rouge officers who had conveniently adopted a pro-Hanoi line when the radical Communist movement split, but both, like Pol Pot, had been in on the brutal social reconstruction of Cambodia that began when the Khmer Rouge took over in 1975 and hundreds of thousands died in macabre executions or from starvation and disease. The Pol Pot faction remained vehemently anti-Vietnamese (and anti-Soviet, or pro-Chinese) and had begun attacking Vietnamese territory in an outburst of irredentism. Hanoi's invasion was therefore strictly an act of self-interest, not a humanitarian gesture, and the Cambodian regime it set up under Heng Samrin and Hun Sen, also heavily supported by Moscow, was never popular. Out of power, the Khmer Rouge continued to stress this theme with some success in its nationalistic propaganda. At his press conference in Bangkok, Gandhi was asked whether India might at some time alter its policy to recognize a broader-based Cambodian government including the resistance, a solution finally brought about by Southeast Asians working through the United Nations and its Security Council members. He gave the question a couple seconds' thought and replied that India's Cambodia policy was something he had inherited from his mother and really had not had time to examine. By contrast, he spoke at length about the technical shortcomings and geopolitical dangers of the American Strategic Defense Initiative known as Star Wars.

With the paucity of information and the lack of debate on foreign affairs in India, and a traditional preference for consensus and a nonpartisan approach to foreign policy, Indians have often been able to delude themselves on international issues, taking positions unsubstantiated by facts and exaggerating their own role in events. This leads to embarrassingly ill-timed gestures by the government, such as bestowing on Yasir Arafat the nation's highest international prize, the Jawaharlal Nehru Award for International Understanding, just as he and the Palestine Liberation Organization appeared to be losing ground in the Middle East, or asserting publicly that Nelson Mandela would make India his first foreign visit after his release from prison to thank Delhi for leading the fight against apartheid. Mandela went to Europe and the United States instead. When he did finally visit India some months later, he drew sparse crowds in most places. Africans, I was told by Indian colleagues, are not very popular in India. When India was threatened for the first time in 1990 with trade sanctions under a retaliatory United States law known as Super 301, the Cabinet of Prime Minister Singh never met to discuss the impending economic crisis or contingency plans for averting or mitigating it, one of his ministers said. Indians largely assumed they were being victimized without cause, and were averse to modifying their ironclad protectionist barriers. Fortunately, the threat just went away, at least temporarily.

Despite a record of false moves or no moves at all, the Indian political and foreign policy establishment, ignoring the country's minuscule contribution to international trade—less than 1 percent in 1991—the shallowness of its national development, and the hundreds of millions of malnourished people living on the edge of subsistence, continues to project India as a power to be reckoned with in the world, morally, economically, and militarily. Ravi Rikhye, a gadfly who likes to disturb the air around sanctified myths, took a sardonic look at this self-image in a fast-paced little book, *The Militarization of Mother India*. "There has never been a case of a country that virtually declares itself a great power, acts like one, but has no strength," he declared. "There is no case where a country expects to be treated like a great power without any of the accouterments of one. No case, that is, until India arrived on the scene." He was writing about the kind of thinking that apparently led K. Subrahmanyam, the country's preeminent strategic analyst, to say without a hint of embarrassment in a "5th Column" guest feature of the *Far Eastern Economic Review* at the beginning of the decade that in the 1990s, "the middle-tier powers like unified Germany, Japan, India, Indonesia, Brazil, Mexico and Canada will play a more significant role." Is there anyone anywhere in the world outside New Delhi who really believes that India is in the same league with Germany or Japan or even Brazil?

"Indian foreign policy must begin to look away from the purely political stance in which Nujoma [the Namibian independence leader], Mandela and Arafat are given more importance than the issues of the global political economy," the public affairs executive (and returned NRI) Rajiv Desai wrote in *The Times of India* in April 1990. "This is not to say that we jettison their causes, but to urge that we take a cold, hard look at current policy, in which the Nonaligned movement secretariat, the United Nations and various other bureaucratic pork barrels are given undue prominence. It is time right-thinking people questioned policies that leave India picking nuts and berries in obscure groves at the margins of the world mainstream." Such calls for a shakeup in Indian foreign policy are beginning to be heard with more frequency in the last decade of the century, some coming for the first time from within the foreign policy establishment itself; for example, in the writings and speeches of A. P. Venkateswaran, a former foreign secretary, the non-political head of the Ministry of External Affairs, and Bhabani Sen Gupta, an author and foreign policy columnist. Venkateswaran says that India has been for too long mesmerized by the concept of nonalignment, as if this commitment alone constituted a foreign policy. Sen Gupta, writing in late September 1991 in *India Abroad*, the parent newspaper of the India Abroad News Service, on a traumatic year in international affairs, denounced a new Indian government for its apparent failure to analyze the rapid changes or conceptualize policy responses. He was contemptuous of the politicians being put in charge of policy at this critical juncture, calling a recently appointed minister of state for external affairs a "slapstick amateur." When this minister, Madhavsinh Solanki, later spoke on foreign policy to a distinguished Asia Society audience in New York, he read from a prepared speech apparently written by someone else and then refused to take any questions. Career Indian foreign service officers shielded him from the knowledgeable audience. He left office soon after, charged by opposition politicians in India with having interfered with Swiss authorities to block an investigation into the Bofors arms scandal. A year later, India scuttled the whole investigation.

Krishnaswami Sunderji, a retired general and former chief of the Indian Army, has also zeroed in on nonalignment. Breaking a taboo against military officers involving themselves in foreign policy, he has on several occasions accused the country's political leadership of forcing the military into "political" conflicts in which they didn't belong: the 1971 Bangladesh war, the 1984 invasion of the Sikhs' Golden Temple in Amritsar, and the 1987 intervention in Sri Lanka. In an interview with *The Times of India* in early 1991, the acerbic General Sunderji had this to say about Indian foreign policy since independence:

> For the past forty years we've had this delightful policy called nonalignment, not only to practice but to use as a crutch, to lean on, to sleep under. It was a very simple policy since your stance, your line, was made for you. All you had to do was mouth platitudes. Such a policy was brought about by a largely bipolar world situation. Now the poles have disappeared and we have been left as waifs and strays as far as foreign policy is concerned. We have got to take a stand and we don't know what to do because we do not have the history or habit of thinking these things through. In foreign and military policy, one should expect a whole spectrum of scenarios from the sublime to the ridiculous, and we should have all the possible answers worked out. That kind of discipline and institutional underpinning is just not there.

Opinions about the world tend to jell quickly in India and are rarely reexamined once formed, as General Sunderji and many others have pointed out. With this in mind, Rama Swarup said, Moscow had invested millions of rupees in holding seminars and financing think tanks or study centers out of funds collected from kickbacks on Soviet-Indian ruble-rupee trade. Hundreds of Indo-Soviet friendship societies and cultural organizations, all financed by Moscow, could also be counted on to disseminate Soviet views. When Ainslie Embree served as counselor for the cultural affairs officer in the United States Embassy in New Delhi from 1978 to 1980, he was frequently approached by Indians wanting to establish Indo-American organizations. They always expected to be given a grant. When told that this was not American policy, their enthusiasm usually waned. When the Soviet Culture Center finally folded in New Delhi in 1992, it had 1,600 Indians on its payroll.

While Swarup did not deny that other nations and international foundations, several in Western Europe, also play roles in supporting cultural or intellectual activities around the world, though not so lavishly, he insisted that Soviet involvement in India was qualitatively different. He said that influential policy institutes were infiltrated, that seminar papers were written in Moscow in "Indian English" for delivery in India, and that a roster of high-ranking Indian officials had been coopted to promote Soviet interests throughout the government. Thousands of students unable to afford a foreign education were given generous scholarships to study in the Soviet Union. On development projects and defense facilities in India, swarms of Soviet technicians were allowed to establish work areas from which Indians were barred. Moscow, Swarup says, systematically used India as a base for infiltration of its ideas into the Third World after it "lost" Belgrade and Cairo. "India had credibility," he said. "No one would have trusted Cuba or North Korea."

Since Indian records are unlikely to be made available, it will be left to historians working with Soviet documents in the post–Cold War era to determine the importance to the wider world of Indian-Soviet cooperation. In the end, New Delhi in its pro-Soviet phase may be judged to have been more of an annoyance or an obstruction than a danger to the West. Ultimately, succeeding Indian governments may have done more to harm the country's reputation than to enhance it during this period. However, a new generation of more sophisticated, more widely traveled, and better informed Indians may find it easier to change or diversify India's orientations in the wake of the collapse of Communism worldwide. In any case, to a diverse collection of republics in what was once the Soviet Union, India may not seem either useful or even relevant any more. By the end of 1991, official India was already talking about the need to integrate itself better into a wider world economy.

Paradoxically, the Indian left—two mainline Communist parties and a host of more radical organizations, some of them armed—were never a crucial factor in Indo-Soviet relations. Indian Communists will argue bitterly that they were in fact marginalized by direct government-to-government and party-to-party links between New Delhi and Moscow. The Indian National Congress and the government it dominated for half a century enjoyed warmer relations with the Soviet leadership than those between the Communist Party of the Soviet Union and leftist parties in India, torn asunder by splits in the 1960s into pro-Soviet and pro-Chinese factions. When Mikhail Gorbachev visited India in 1988, his second official trip to Delhi, he did not meet with the Indian Communist leadership, which had become critical of both his open personal style and his fundamental reforms. Sitting under their portraits of Stalin, aging Indian Communists accused him of iconoclasm, heresy, and pandering to the Americans. They were incensed that he took his well-dressed wife, Raisa, everywhere he went; a Western public relations stunt, they called it. The truth seemed to be that Gorbachev, or any other Soviet leader, never really needed them.

The debate is only beginning over what kind of impact, if any, the bear hug of Soviet friendship had on Indians outside official and intellectual circles, that vast and silent majority increasingly out of line with the interests of the government. For most, it might be assumed there was no impact at all, although some Indians argue that years of Soviet-supported socialist planning, the penchant for giant projects at the expense of village-scale development, and the nationalization of financial institutions and strategic industries—Indian policies strengthened by Soviet advice and example—left India poorer, prolonging the deprivation of millions. Consumer products were late to develop and were largely uncompetitive in markets outside the needy Soviet bloc because of their inferior quality. By 1988, when the faltering Soviet economy was under pressure to improve the standards and supply of consumer goods, Moscow's trade experts were lecturing their Indian counterparts on quality control. Even India's lucrative trade with the Soviet Union seemed in jeopardy.

Other Indians who have been jailed and tortured on subversion charges are convinced that methods of interrogation and sometimes torture instruments used on them (identified by their cyrillic markings) were Soviet, although brutality in Indian jails is common and there are plenty of locally contrived abuses, including the application of the "roller" that exerts unbearable pressure on the muscles and bones as it moves up and down the leg under the weight of up to four men, the barbaric blinding of prisoners, and the routine raping of female inmates. Simranjit Singh Mann, a Sikh political leader and former high-ranking police official who was jailed for five years on unsubstantiated charges of involvement in the conspiracy to assassinate Indira Gandhi, says he is certain from both his professional work and his experience in jail that Indian law enforcement agencies used Soviet interrogation techniques and equipment. Mann emerged from prison in 1989 with considerable physical and psychological damage though he had never been convicted of a crime.

Leaders of the Ananda Marga, part cult and part anti-Communist self-help development organization, which was hounded for years by the Communist-led government of West Bengal state, make similar accusations of Soviet-style persecution. In early 1990, Patricia Munday, an American who had joined the Ananda Marga sect at a commune in Vermont, was attacked by local cadre of the Communist Party of India—Marxist (the CPM to Indians) while traveling with another foreigner in the West Bengal coun-

tryside, near the group's international headquarters at Purulia. Munday, an
emergency medical technician who had been part of a United Nations High
Commissioner for Refugees team that won a Nobel Peace Prize for work in
Somalia in 1982, was clubbed with a brick and had her passport and other
valuables stolen before being picked up by the police. She and half a dozen
other foreigners were thrown in a van the next day and taken to Calcutta,
the West Bengal capital, where police officers taunted her about being a CIA
spy and tried to have her deported, saying she did not have an Indian visa—
a charge she denied but could not disprove without her passport. She was
held under guard in a state government guest house and then a Calcutta
nursing home, unable to make a telephone call, for two weeks. West Bengal
state's government was led by Chief Minister Jyoti Basu, an urbane septuge-
narian frequently described as one of the most pragmatic and democratic of
Indian Communists.

When I met Munday later at New Delhi's All India Institute of Medical
Sciences, where she had been moved after the intercession of lawyers who
had gone to the Supreme Court of India to secure a deportation stay order so
that she could leave India by her own decision and later return to fight her
case, she was in a dank, dismal room, watched over by a sullen policeman
slumped in a chair. Another police officer was posted outside the door.

Munday was no stranger to India. "I had been a kind of seeker," she
said. "I had studied in Madras. I had looked all over India for a guru. I had
read them all. But it was in Vermont that I met these people doing social
service. I was attracted to their belief that you follow the path of bliss by
both meditation and service to others. Why was there so much violence in
Bengal? I think it was because we believed that first you give people food
and shelter and access to medicine, and then you give them education so
that they'll be free, and not so vulnerable to politicians. In West Bengal, the
Communists were breaking down our schools and hospitals because they
were a threat. This is a small world and we are all interconnected. But truth,
justice—the American way—it doesn't quite work that way elsewhere."
Twenty-four-hours later, United States officials helped Munday on a plane
home at her request. "I thought India and America had good relations," she
said before she left. "What happened to me should be a warning to everybody."

Indo-Soviet cooperation in intelligence and law enforcement sometimes
worked both ways. In the late 1980s, Soviet policemen were being sent to
India to learn crowd control. And as for surveillance, the dissemination of
disinformation, and what the Calcutta editor and writer Sunanda K. Datta-
Ray calls the practice of "drawing room duplicity" in foreign affairs, the
Indians may have been able to teach their Soviet friends some lessons. Indians were masters of such skills by the fourth century B.C. when a Brahmin
minister to the Emperor Chandragupta Maurya perfected the art of out-
foxing aliens. The minister, known variously to historians as Kautilya,

Chanakya, or sometimes Vishnugupta, was the author (or one of the authors) of the *Arthasastra,* a guide to statecraft and kingship that was a model of Realpolitik centuries before the birth of Machiavelli. To achieve unity within the state and dominance over its neighbors, Kautilya advocated treachery, extensive espionage, the use of *agents provocateurs,* fraud, rumormongering, forgeries, poison, torture, and the ruthless use of force when necessary.

Diplomats based in New Delhi, subject to surveillance and daily minor irritations born of the arrogance of foreign policymakers in the Ministry of External Affairs, note wryly that it is not lost on them that India chose to call its diplomatic enclave Chanakyapuri and name a major road through it Kautilya Marg. "The Soviet way of doing things influenced the Indians because they fitted in to the Indian way of doing things," Ainslie Embree speculated. Embree, who taught at an Indian college from 1948 to 1958, continues in retirement to promote scholarly exchanges with India, not always an easy task in a country that is very suspicious of foreign experts. Even American graduate students are warned against trying to do field research in India on sensitive topics. Indian delays in issuing visas or outright rejection of applications make scholarly study of India, particularly in the humanities and social sciences, difficult. Americans, discouraged by New Delhi's uncooperative attitude toward research, often leave the field for studies in other Asian areas. So few Americans study in India compared with the number of Indians going to the United States that Embree says exchange programs have become so asymmetrical that they can hardly be described as exchange programs at all. This seems to satisfy those Indian intellectuals worried about what they call academic imperialism. In their rush to protect themselves from foreign influence, Indians are limiting knowledge of and appreciation for India the world over.

When Indians agonize over how and why they allowed themselves to be overrun and dominated by outsiders for so many years before regaining independence in 1947, they sometimes recall the lessons of Kautilya, who warned among other things that disunity within a realm made it vulnerable, whatever its military strength. Such an admonition contributes to the obsession with preserving at any cost the geographical and cultural integrity of India, and to the policy of covering up international embarrassments with elaborate propaganda facades. In 1991, the official attempt to rewrite the story of what happened in a hamlet called Kunan Poshpora, near the Pakistan border in Kashmir, was a classic example of the genre. The people of Kunan Poshpora say that on a night in February of that year, troops from the Indian Army seized their village, confined the men, and raped dozens of women—the number varies, and was no doubt embellished over time. Kashmiri human rights monitors and journalists—including Christopher Thomas of *The Times* of London—hiked to the hamlet to hear the accounts first hand. Thomas said that there was no doubt in his mind that there had been a mass sexual assault; only some of the details were in question. Several foreign news organizations in New Delhi, among them the BBC and *The New York Times,* had obtained a local magistrate's report that described the offending troops as "beasts."

The Indian government, stung by accusations made not against more unruly paramilitary forces but soldiers of the Rajputana Rifles, mounted a prolonged campaign to discredit both the villagers of Kunan Poshpora and the foreign and Indian reporters who had written about their accusations. A committee of the Press Council of India was taken to the hamlet by the Indian Army and presented with the same fallacious "facts" intended to undermine the credibility of the victims that Jammu and Kashmir's governor, Girish Saxena, a former head of the foreign intelligence service, the Research and Analysis Wing, had pressed on foreign correspondents. The Press Council team—which included a distinguished writer, George Verghese, who had been balanced in his reporting on Kashmir in the past—collected inconclusive evidence but concluded anyway that the people of Kunan Poshpora had been lying. No journalist familiar with the Kashmir Valley was not pained to see this travesty published purely in the interests of clearing the Indian Army's name.

In domestic politics, numerous Kautilyan arts enjoyed a revival under recent Congress Party governments, beginning with the first administration of Indira Gandhi, when her late son Sanjay, never a democrat by instinct, was her closest political adviser. Spies and *agents provocateurs* operated extensively and freely at home and abroad under Indira Gandhi and her eventual successor, her elder son, Rajiv, who also used the national Intelligence Bureau for political opinion polling and the foreign intelligence agency, the Research and Analysis Wing, for attempts to subvert secessionist movements in restive states. Agents of various services apparently infiltrated opposition groups and staged acts of violence intended to appear the work of militants. Rebellious Sikhs in Punjab are convinced that the conservative journalist Dhiren Bhagat was murdered, not killed accidentally in a car crash, after he revealed in 1988 in a column in *The Bombay Post* and *The Observer* in London that the Research and Analysis Wing had been smuggling arms from Afghanistan to India. Officials denied the accusation and Bhagat's friends discount a conspiracy, saying that he was always a reckless driver. What aroused suspicions in Punjab, however, was that Bhagat had speculated that the weapons would be planted on Sikh separatists or used in Punjab by double agents so that the government could claim sophisticated arms from the Afghan war were turning up in India. In a subsequent article by Bhagat, now part of the collection of his writings published posthumously as *The Contemporary Conservative,* the journalist detailed how the government of Rajiv Gandhi tried to discredit him and cover up his story before having to admit that at least one consignment of arms had indeed arrived under false documentation.

In Canada the following year, two journalists, Zuhair Kashmeri of the *Globe and Mail* and Brian McAndrew of the *Toronto Star,* released a book, *Soft Target,* that argued (persuasively but not decisively) that Indian intelligence agents operating in Canada had planned the 1985 bombing of the Air India jet *Kanishka* over the North Atlantic, in which 329 people died. The motive, they said, was to discredit the Sikhs, who were becoming a large and influential minority in Canada. Indian officials have dismissed the conclusion of these investigative journalists as preposterous. Sikh leaders in the United States and Canada are divided on the conclusions of *Soft Target,* but are convinced that Indian diplomats in North America are trying to turn public and official opinion against Sikhs because many, though far from all, of them are openly campaigning and raising money for an independent homeland they call Khalistan. Increasingly, Kashmiris living abroad say that they are facing some of the same tensions and threats from Indian government agents or other Indians acting on Delhi's behalf. Immigration lawyers in New York find that Sikhs seeking asylum on legitimate fears of persecution or death in India rarely get strong support from State Department officials, who tend to accept Indian government claims that all or most Sikhs fleeing India are terrorists. Attitudes among diplomats are changing, however, as human rights abuses on both sides of the civil strife in Punjab become more widely publicized and better documented, and as Sikh groups in Canada and the United States improve and expand their legislative lobbies.

In mid-August 1989, a few months before a national election, backers of Prime Minister Rajiv Gandhi, who appeared likely to be defeated in his bid for reelection, made an astonishingly inept attempt to discredit his rival and former colleague, Vishwanath Pratap Singh, through the release to the international and national press of letters they had apparently forged to implicate Singh in an illegal bank account in the Caribbean. The fraudulent letters and documents, so clumsily crafted as to be doubted on sight, purported to show that Singh's son Ajeya, then living in Connecticut, had opened a multimillion-dollar account with the First Trust Corporation Limited of St. Kitts and Nevis and made his father beneficiary. The elder Singh was supposed to have deposited $21 million in the account while he was finance minister of India, and withdrawn sums ranging between $2 million and $5 million from 1986 until early 1988 after he had left the government and been expelled from the Congress Party.

Copies of these documents were supplied to *The New York Times* not in New Delhi, where the Singh family immediately challenged them as frauds, but in Washington. The courier was Larry Kolb, a stepson-in-law of the international arms dealer and financier Adnan Khashoggi, whose residential fax number appeared at the top of each page of material sent to *The Times.* Kolb, who was subsequently named by officials in India for his role in the affair, told a *Times* reporter in Washington that his motive in sharing this information with the paper was helping Rajiv Gandhi get reelected. The alert reporter passed the "documents" on to New York for forwarding to Delhi. Other foreign publications, including *The Observer* in London, received similar packets of "documents" and did not use them, but some papers rushed into print without making any effort to check the material. The fabricated story was published as fact by *The Arab Times* in Kuwait and *Golge Adam* in Istanbul, and clippings of those articles were circulated by Khashoggi's office to lend credence to the phony documents. The Press Trust of India circulated the *Arab Times* version, but the story was also published independently in India, most prominently (but without a byline) in *The Telegraph* of Calcutta, whose editor, M. J. Akbar, was a Rajiv Gandhi crony and later member of Parliament and spokesman for the Congress Party. *The Hindustan Times* ran the story without the knowledge of its editor, H. K. Dua, who had gone home for the day when the news suddenly "broke." Dua, a distinguished journalist of long experience, was angry and offered to resign but was persuaded by the newspaper's owners, the Birla industrial family, to stay. It was later reported in India that the St. Kitts story had been planted over Dua's head by aides in the prime minister's office. As elsewhere, politicians in India cultivate good relationships with major newspapers.

The only newspaper to investigate the St. Kitts charges thoroughly, and convincingly expose them as fraudulent, was not an Indian publication but the New York weekly *India Abroad*, edited and published by Gopal Raju, a South Indian long settled in the United States. In a series of important articles that deserved far greater attention than they got worldwide, the reporter Lynn Hudson followed the story from Basseterre, the capital of St. Kitts and Nevis, where he found the bank in question now defunct and replaced by a boutique, through Miami to sources in New York, London, and Canada, where he discovered that some investors and officers of the First Trust Corporation were suspected of (and later charged with) laundering drug money.

India Abroad reported that P. V. Narasimha Rao, foreign minister at the time and later prime minister, had ordered India's consul general in New York, Rajendra Kumar Rai, to notarize or "authenticate" the signature of a former managing director of the First Trust Corporation, George D. McLean, who had attested to the validity of the forged documents. The consul general had never met McLean when he duly certified that the verifying signature on the forgeries was true. India's ambassador in Washington at the time, the Hindu prince Karan Singh, the last maharaja of Kashmir, responded to the protests of Indian-Americans with the weak excuse that Rai had merely authenticated the signatures, not the fraudulent information in the papers they contained. Indian residents feared the precedent that had been set by this political interference in the functioning of diplomats, and charged that the rights of Ajeya Singh, an American resident but Indian passport holder, had been violated. *India Abroad* also reported that the Central Bureau of

Investigation, India's FBI, had been involved in promoting the false charges against V. P. Singh and his son, and that the CBI's director of enforcement, A. P. Nanday, had personally taken the bogus papers to Consul General Rai in New York to be notarized. A CBI indictment a year later, when V. P. Singh was prime minister and the scandal was briefly investigated, mentioned that Nanday had traveled from St. Kitts to New York on a private plane owned by Khashoggi. In India, only *The Indian Express*, then under the editorship of Arun Shourie, a foe of the Gandhi administration, used the *India Abroad* reports prominently and by special arrangement, since the *Express* did not subscribe to the India Abroad News Service.

The St. Kitts forgeries were exposed in August and September 1989, but the enemies of V. P. Singh did not abandon their fraudulent tactics. In November, shortly before the national election, Subramaniam Swamy, a political chameleon with a taste for publicity, produced what he said were documents proving that Singh had a link with the CIA. The bogus evidence included a purported cable from the New Delhi American Embassy to the CIA and the State Department, and a concocted letter to a phony CIA agent from The Committee for the Free World, a right-wing organization whose director was then Midge Decter. The letter, informing a "Richard Mitchell, Esq." that his (the CIA's) request for a million-dollar "grant" to V. P. Singh had been approved, was signed "Irv," apparently intended to mean Irving Kristol, the conservative writer, who was a Committee member. Within hours, the CIA and the State Department denounced the documents as absolute forgeries, and friends of Kristol, who never signed himself "Irv," said that handwriting in the signature was not his. When I spoke by telephone from Delhi with Decter in New York, she dismissed the whole attempt as so ridiculous as to border on the humorous. The Committee for the Free World letterhead used by the forgers was nearly a decade out of date and had been long ago discarded by the organization. Five board members listed on the letterhead brandished by Swamy (who has a Harvard degree) were no longer in office; one had died five years earlier. In the United States, Senator Daniel Patrick Moynihan, the New York Democrat and former ambassador to India, called the forgeries "contemptible." Speaking in the Senate on November 20, almost on the eve of voting in India, Moynihan said: "I am sure that the electorate of the world's largest democracy will not let their votes be affected by a transparent and pitiable fraud. Pitiable but no less despicable." Only in a country as out of touch with the world and as bereft of ethical accountability as India would such an absurd set of forgeries get so much attention.

Vishwanath Pratap Singh, a man of unchallenged integrity, was never damaged by the attempted forgeries, however. He went on to win the election, though with his new Janata Dal party and its larger National Front coalition in a minority position in Parliament. Asked about the episode in several subsequent interviews he always laughed off the bungled scandal, saying that "the Congress Party has a whole department of forgeries." The affair did not significantly damage the political fortunes of the perpetrators of the frauds either, affirming public perceptions that in Indian politics, anything goes. No heads rolled in the Rajiv Gandhi camp for these embarrassing failures; principles and ethics were again not issues. India would have no Watergate. Subramaniam Swamy was part of the cabal that later brought down V. P. Singh by splitting his party; he was rewarded by being named commerce minister in the Chandra Shekhar administration. The official investigation into the plot soon went into drift, as most investigations do in India, even though charges had been filed by the Central Bureau of Intelligence. The ubiquitous and powerful guru to the rich and famous, Chandraswamy, who also had a hand in the affair, evaded arrest, and no official was able to explain the active participation of Khashoggi, who was then also involved in defending himself against charges, later dropped, of fronting for Ferdinand and Imelda Marcos in property deals in New York.

Michael Hershman, who heads the Fairfax Group, a private international investigation agency in Fairfax, Virgina, which had done some work for the Indian government when V. P. Singh was finance minister, has a theory. In an interview a year after the St. Kitts affair, he said that Khashoggi's interest was not in Indian politics, "except to get a government elected that would give him contracts." Hershman described Khashoggi as a "five percenter" who had made a fortune in commissions on the sale of arms and other equipment in the Middle East. He was eventually cut out of lucrative Saudi deals, Hershman said, and then lost money on real estate projects in the United States. Hershman thought that Khashoggi was merely looking for new countries in which to do business, and was using Chandraswamy, a guru popular with politicians, as a way to meet the right people. Hershman also said that Khashoggi would have helped either Rajiv Gandhi or Chandra Shekhar in 1989 in order to prevent V. P. Singh from taking power. Singh had made his reputation as a "clean" finance minister who wanted to root out decisively the system of paying commissions on government contracts, which is in theory illegal in India. Hershman said that he or his associates met Khashoggi or members of his team "six to eight times" in 1988 and 1989 at the request of the arms dealer to discuss possible investigations into the records of leading Indian politicians before it occurred to Hershman and his Fairfax colleagues that Khashoggi was hoping to draw them into plots to discredit Singh. In India, Hershman's word would have carried considerable weight since he had known Singh and worked for him. But Hershman said that he made his own inquiries into the St. Kitts affair and saw there was no basis for what he called "the Ajeya ploy." He told Khashoggi he would not get involved in such an investigation. "I said, look, there is just no way," he recalled.

In early 1991, two Indian governments later, Khashoggi made a quick and flamboyant visit to Delhi by private plane. A roster of important Indians—including Rajiv Gandhi, Prime Minister Chandra Shekhar, Chandras-wamy, and several prominent business leaders—lined up to talk or dine with him, undeterred by the public impression this created. The spectacle moved Dileep Padgaonkar, editor of *The Times of India*, to write a signed editorial that said: "The fawning on Mr. Khashoggi is only symptomatic of what happens to an elite when its moral fibre is coarsened, its self-respect is eroded, its faith in reasoned debate is shaken and its democratic spirit is debased." In India, he said, "once cash flows, conviction follows."

10

India and Its Neighbors

SEEN FROM AFAR, WHERE, the historian Romila Thapar says, Western Orientalists cast an aura "fragrant with exotica" around India, this large nation remains a land of romance, drama, and deep spirituality. It can be all of those things, and more. Indians inhabit spectacular landscapes, they dress effortlessly in colors and patterns and styles of arresting attraction. And since nothing is discarded, ancient culture flourishes all around them. But seen from a closer vantage point, from the smaller nations that must live perennially in India's shadow, this mammoth land is not a gallery of glories but a source of insecurity and a massive stumbling block to regional development. Because of India's overwhelming presence and its penchant for micromanaging regional affairs, no major development takes place without Indian approval or involvement. India has opposed all efforts by Bangladesh to promote international management of the huge river systems that perennially threaten that small nation. The example of the international Mekong River basin commission in Southeast Asia is often cited but never emulated. Nepal, China, India, and Bangladesh all have a role to play in the future of the Ganges and Brahmaputra watersheds, but New Delhi wants to deal with one capital at a time so that India's interests are always paramount, whether or not this hastens ecological disaster. Meanwhile, Bangladeshi doctors are looking at a new medical phenomenon among children that they call the Farakka Syndrome, named for an Indian dam on the Ganges that they say has altered the level and salinity of water downstream in Bangladesh significantly enough to cause health problems.

For decades, India also blocked or discouraged the establishment of non-

stop air connections between Delhi and the neighboring capitals of Colombo, Dhaka, and Islamabad, and strictly limited the number of Indian
airports where foreign flights may land or the routes they may fly, greatly
restricting business and tourism within the region—a situation Southeast
Asians would not tolerate. Indian officials argue that the capital-to-capital
routes are not viable, but never explain why Indian Airlines (the over-
stretched domestic carrier, which also serves the region) could not emulate
Pakistan International's smooth service to Islamabad through Lahore, with
only a brief stopover to clear customs and immigration. Indian Airlines
could, but for years did not, introduce similar direct flights from Delhi to
Dhaka or Colombo with an intermediary Indian stop that does not require
the almost inevitable overnight stay in Calcutta, Madras, or Trivandrum.
Improbable as it looks on the map, the fastest and most reliable journey to
Sri Lanka or Bangladesh, business travelers have discovered, is usually
through Bangkok, more than a thousand miles out of the way but light years
ahead in efficiency and service.

Politically, every one of India's smaller neighbors has been the victim of
Kautilyan intrigue since the death of Nehru in 1964 and the subsequent
consolidation of power by his daughter, Indira Gandhi, a few years later.
Except for two brief historical moments in 1977–79 under a Janata Party
government and in 1989–90 when Prime Minister Vishwanath Pratap Singh
and his foreign minister, Inder Kumar Gujral, pledged to stop playing dirty
tricks on the neighbors, Indian policymaking on Sri Lanka, Bangladesh, Nepal, Bhutan, and to some extent Maldives and Pakistan (a special case) was a
game for intelligence agents, schemers in the Ministry of External Affairs,
and viceregal diplomats in imperial cloaks.

One country, the Kingdom of Sikkim, disappeared entirely in the mid-
1970s, swallowed by India after its ethnic unity and peace were destroyed in
a ruthless campaign of destabilization. The sad story has been extensively
documented and effectively written by the journalist Sunanda K. Datta-Ray
in his 1984 book, *Smash and Grab: Annexation of Sikkim*. Not content with
having abolished the throne of the Sikkimese ruler, Chogyal Tenzing
Topgyal Wangchuck Sisum Namgyal, Indira Gandhi's agents hounded the
deposed king until his death from cancer in New York in 1982. One of his
sins had been marrying an American, Hope Cooke, who Indians whispered
was a CIA agent in disguise, and whom many Sikkimese still regard as a
dangerously naive young woman who took up too publicly the cause of
Sikkimese nationalism and thereby added to the provocations India needed
to rob the nation of its independence. When the former Chogyal came to
dinner at Datta-Ray's Calcutta home after the annexation, Indian policemen
evicted a German diplomatic couple who had come to say goodbye. To
complete the humiliation, the police also followed the monarch, broken in
health and spirit, to the bathroom. "This shy, sad man with his gentle ways
and crippling stammer, his soft speech and quiet thoughtfulness, was lost to

view under an avalanche of pejorative propaganda," Datta-Ray wrote by way of epitaph. An Indian official who figured in the story tried unsuccessfully to stop the publication of *Smash and Grab*, dampening the enthusiasm of the publisher. The book is now out of print in India, but I found it displayed prominently in the best bookshop in the small Sikkimese capital, Gangtok, a reminder of the quiet resentment still felt by many Sikkimese. "The Indians took our country and then made sure there would be no opposition by pouring in money to corrupt as many people as possible," a Sikkimese living in neighboring Nepal said. "All the development you see is there to buy us off."

The story of Sikkim is seared on the minds of the Bhutanese, people of the same Tibetan Buddhist beliefs and ethnic stock as the native Sikkimese. A fast-growing Nepali-speaking minority in the small Kingdom of Bhutan, augmented by illegal immigrants from Nepal and Nepali-speaking areas of India, threatens to develop into the same kind of fifth column that served to bring about the fall of the Sikkimese monarchy. The Royal Bhutanese government, under King Jigme Singye Wangchuck, has gone out of its way not to upset India, so that history will not repeat itself. The Indians have been allowed to erect an incongruously huge embassy in the tiny Bhutanese capital of Thimpu, and there is a highly visible Indian military presence in the hills and valleys of this unspoiled mountain kingdom, which borders China. The troops are there ostensibly to train the minuscule Bhutanese army and oversee development projects; any tourist can see them on the roads, and their commander rates VIP treatment at the little international airport at Paro, yet Indian officials sometimes deny that they have soldiers in Bhutan when talking to Delhi-based diplomats. India expects to be called on first when Bhutan needs a foreign expert in industry, government, or the arts, whether or not Delhi's candidate is the right person for the job. Incompetent advisers seem to be legion, to judge from Bhutanese accounts. Bhutan has never established full diplomatic relations with the United States, so that there can be no accusation of deviation from Indian policy lines or fears that this harmless little realm will be used as a base against India, as Sikkim was thought to be with Hope Cooke and her American friends coming and going from New York and Washington before she deserted Sikkim and the Chogyal in 1974. A Bhutanese official, talking candidly about the parameters in which Bhutan must operate internationally, recalled how a Cuban diplomat had once been deputed to warn Thimpu when it strayed toward a Western point of view on an issue of importance to India being debated at the United Nations.

It was Nepal's turn to feel the wrath of India in 1989–1990, when New Delhi imposed tough economic sanctions on its small landlocked neighbor and hastened its slide into political crisis. Indian and Nepali officials offer an interesting array of explanations for what triggered the confrontation. Nepal and India had since 1950 been bound by a treaty of friendship that New

Delhi said Kathmandu had been violating by requiring Indians to have work permits in Nepal while Nepalis entered India to work without them, and by imposing tariffs on some Indian goods. Nepal had also been awarding development projects to Chinese contractors and had bought anti-aircraft weapons from Beijing without India's permission. India's External Affairs Ministry was annoyed that electronic goods and other items that could not be imported into India because of protectionist policies were being smuggled across the border from Nepal, along with some cheap Chinese consumer goods. "You can have a VCR from Hong Kong delivered to your door in Patna," an Indian diplomat remarked in annoyance to demonstrate the mockery made of Indian laws. Indian goods, on the other hand, flooded the shops of Kathmandu, stifling the development of local products. Much of the smuggled foreign merchandise—from Japan, Hong Kong, Singapore, and the West—for sale in Nepal was, in any case, sold by Indians to other Indians, since Nepalis could not afford these luxuries. An Indian clientele also dominated the slot machines and gaming tables of the exquisitely declasse casino at the Soaltee Oberoi hotel, where shrieking children raced around and greasy samosas on paper plates got trampled underfoot.

Nepal's view of the dispute, outlined by the foreign minister at the time, Shailendra Kumar Upapahyay, was that India wanted Kathmandu to repent and retreat on relations with China, and was bent on consolidating the kingdom's two major commercial treaties with New Delhi—one on trade and one guaranteeing landlocked Nepal's transit rights through Indian territory. Nepal considered transit a subject under international jurisdiction, protected by covenants accepted worldwide, and wanted this treaty to remain separate from that on bilateral trade. Kathmandu had enjoyed this arrangement since 1978, when the Janata Party government of Morarji Desai granted the concession of separate treaties that had been denied by Congress Party regimes. Calcutta is the mountain kingdom's closest port, and all goods are carried to and from the docks or Indian railheads overland by truck, since Nepal has no railways to connect the Kathmandu Valley to the sea. A guaranteed right of transit is essential. The trade and transit treaties, which had lapsed, were redrawn late in 1988 and initialed by both sides. Then in early 1989, India inexplicably reneged on signing them and furthermore allowed two additional bilateral agreements to run out, covering supplies of petroleum and coal to Nepal from or through India. By the end of March 1989, India had closed all but two border-crossing points to Nepali commerce and simultaneously slashed its fuel supplies.

That was the public part of the squabble. Unofficially, both Nepali and Indian diplomats and policymakers said, the "frosty" relationship between Prime Minister Rajiv Gandhi and King Birendra Bir Bikram Shah Dev of Nepal—two image-conscious and reasonably uncharitable men—had played a big part in the drama. The mutual irritation peaked during a summit meeting of the seven-nation South Asian Association for Regional Cooperation in Islamabad in December 1988. Indians say that King Birendra snubbed a breakfast invitation from Gandhi; Nepalis say that the king refused to be photographed with Gandhi and the King of Bhutan, who many Nepalis thought had allowed himself to be treated as a vassal of Imperial India. Whatever really happened in Islamabad, it was King Birendra who would ultimately be the loser, not the people of Nepal. They proved to be more resilient under Indian pressure than New Delhi apparently expected. A year of hardship and mounting political protest, some of it openly backed by Indian politicians who came to Nepal and made public speeches against royalty, followed. The crisis peaked in early 1990 in street demonstrations suppressed by the Royal government, with the Nepali left and the Indian press greatly inflating the casualties for world consumption. To avoid further violence, the Nepali monarch was forced to abdicate much of his absolute power in new constitution, and Nepal was on its way to its first democratic election in more than three decades.

What New Delhi had not anticipated was the ability of the Nepali people to separate their grievances against the king from their attitudes toward India, which they believed had now openly demonstrated its willingness to strip Nepal of sovereignty—if it was not in a position to annex the country outright—through economic sanctions and diplomatic arm-twisting. The resurgent Nepali left made the most of this anti-Indian sentiment in the 1991 national election. India had failed in its primary aims: to consolidate the trade and transit treaties and curtail the influence of China in Nepal. In 1990, another non-Congress government under V. P. Singh, overriding efforts by its own foreign ministry to sabotage the bettering of relations with Kathmandu, signed the two new treaties Nepal wanted. Most other outstanding differences were also resolved by India's pragmatic foreign minister, Inder Kumar Gujral, and Nepal's acting prime minister, Krishna Prasad Bhattarai, eliminating much of the pressure on this small country trying to recover from both political turbulence and economic dislocation. Meanwhile, Nepal successfully broadened its trade links in Asia, expanded the number of foreign airlines flying directly to Kathmandu, bypassing India, and resumed giving large construction contracts to the Chinese. The crucial Nepali tourist industry, damaged by the fuel crisis and street violence, soon began to recover. Because charming little Nepal has many fans around the world, India's image took an unexpected beating.

"Even with the damage repaired, we have lost the trust and confidence of the Nepali people," the foreign policy analyst Bhabani Sen Gupta said in an interview after the settlement of the crisis. "Our special relationship with Nepal is dead. They will not trust us with their water resources, which are important to us. Bangladesh has the same attitude. We have done no homework on our relationships in the region. We need new neighborhood policies; for too long our relationships have been victims of adhocism, with no constructive ideas coming from India, the natural regional leader." Sen

Gupta believed that a renewed fear of China, more than the trade issues or hostility to King Birendra, was the primary cause of New Delhi's overreaction to Nepal's small steps toward asserting itself. Nepal formed a corridor from Chinese Tibet into the heart of India, and by 1989, Sen Gupta said, Moscow had made it clear to India that it could expect no assistance if New Delhi got into another conflict with Beijing. But for more than a quarter of a century, Indian policies have been pushing regional nations closer to the Chinese, who cannot ignore New Delhi's repeated interventions in neighbors' affairs. "China doesn't assume automatically that India should enjoy hegemony in South Asia," Sen Gupta said. "When neighbors of India cry out, China cannot dismiss them."

He mentioned Sri Lanka, which, like Nepal, Pakistan, and Bangladesh, was turning to China for weapons. Over the 1980s, Colombo had been confronted by a mushrooming Tamil insurgency supported by India. Sri Lankan or "Jaffna" Tamils, a linguistic-cultural minority of about 12 percent concentrated for many centuries in the island's north and east, began their separatist campaign against Colombo after the country's Sinhala-speaking majority eroded their rights, marginalized their language, and finally attacked their homes and livelihoods. These Jaffna Tamils, the majority of them Hindus but with a substantial number of Christians among them, were a skilled community. Many had been educated in Jaffna by American missionaries and were able to corner a disproportionately large percentage of jobs in the professions and civil service before Sri Lanka became independent in 1948. Many others took their skills to other outposts of the British Empire in Asia, becoming lawyers and doctors in Singapore and Kuala Lumpur, for example. The Jaffna Tamils are a distinct Sri Lankan community, different in history and caste from the "Indian" Tamils, the laborers brought by the British to the tea plantations in the central hills of what was then Ceylon in the nineteenth and early twentieth centuries. The descendants of those tea plantation workers, now about seven or eight percent of the Sri Lankan population, live surrounded by Sinhalese and have not joined the Tamil freedom movement. The Jaffna Tamils, however, were far away from the centers of Sinhalese life, and close to India's Tamil Nadu state where, beginning in the 1980s, they began to find sanctuary, then training and arms.

Indian officials no longer deny that Indira Gandhi at some point decided that a serious Tamil insurrection in Sri Lanka would serve her interests. Gandhi had been close to Sirimavo Bandaranaike, the prime minister whose Sri Lankan Freedom Party moved the country sharply to the left in the 1960s and 1970s through nationalizations, the closing of Christian schools, and a lot of anti-Western political rhetoric, while—ironically in the light of subsequent events—institutionalizing Sinhalese dominance at the expense of the Tamil minority. Bandaranaike's assassinated husband, Prime Minister Solomon W. R. D. Bandaranaike, had been the author of the 1956 law making

Sinhala the sole national language. Sirimavo Bandaranaike was defeated in 1977, and Sri Lanka began to swing back toward the right in economic and foreign policies under Junius Richard Jayewardene, prime minister and then president after a new constitution was introduced in 1978. But right or left, Sri Lanka had in a few decades become South Asia's model developing nation, with a literacy rate over 90 percent, extensive welfare programs, and one of the lowest population growth rates in Asia. Indira Gandhi did not like what she saw. Sri Lanka had begun to look like a conduit for Western influence in the region. Gandhi also had a visceral dislike for Jayewardene, who later told me in an interview how difficult it was to work with her, and how distrustful he was of her intentions. It was a well placed fear. One of her aides recalled that she was once heard to say: "I'm going to get that old man."

Within a few years of Indira Gandhi's return to power in 1980 after two years out of office, India had as a matter of policy begun to arm and train several of Sri Lanka's Tamil guerrilla groups. The most ruthless and skilled of the lot were the Liberation Tigers of Tamil Eelam who, by the late 1980s, were in virtual control of the Jaffna peninsula and large areas of northern and eastern Sri Lanka. The Tigers were led by Velupillai Prabakaran, a single-minded fanatic from a low-caste fishing family whom Indian diplomats would later call a fascist. For years, however, he was India's man. The late Harry Jayewardene, the president's brother and leader of a Sri Lankan delegation to peace talks with several rebel groups in 1985, told me afterwards that Prabakaran arrived for the talks, held in the Bhutanese capital, Thimphu, in the company of Indian intelligence handlers from the Research and Analysis Wing. When in New Delhi, the Tigers' leader was lodged as an official guest in the government-owned luxury hotel, the Ashoka.

The Tamil guerrillas were also supported by governments of Tamil Nadu state in the name of Tamil chauvinism and kinship. In the '80s, the administration of a former film star, Chief Minister M. G. Ramachandran, allowed the Sri Lanka rebels free run of the city of Madras and the Coromandel coast stretching to the south, where at one point only eighteen miles of shallow water separates India from Sri Lanka. Camps were set up inland by Indian intelligence and military officers. According to Indian journalists, the scale and thoroughness of the project to undermine Sri Lanka far outshone anything Pakistan has done recently in support of the Kashmiri rebellion, yet India was never challenged in international organizations, or in the United States Congress, which could have invoked aid sanctions intended for countries that actively seek to destabilize other friendly nations. The foreign policy analyst Bhabani Sen Gupta called the Indian policy "a classic case of intervention," and Sri Lankans interpret the American silence as proof that Washington had turned the region over to India. American officials say that there was very little leverage the United States could have brought to bear on India, since aid was minimal and New Delhi was not a major purchaser of military equipment—an argument also offered for why Indian nuclear development does not come in for the same harsh scrutiny in Washington as the Pakistani program. Indeed, the level of American high technology shared with India rose dramatically in the mid-to-late 1980s, and New Delhi was able to obtain a Cray "supercomputer."

The Colombo government, calling in vain for outside diplomatic help, began to expand its armed forces and prepare a ground war to dislodge the insurgents. As the campaign intensified, both sides demonstrated that they were capable of the most brutal abuses against civilian populations that got in the way or, increasingly on the Tigers' part, were not sufficiently loyal. People were shot in their homes, blown up by land mines, and pulled off buses to be murdered for speaking the wrong language. Sri Lanka's Muslim minority, which considers itself a longstanding separate ethnic group once called the Ceylon Moors, suffered multiple atrocities as they tried to remain independent of both sides. In its fight to save the territorial integrity of the country, the Sri Lankan government sought and got military equipment from Pakistan and China; it got intelligence assistance from Israel and private British counterinsurgency experts. Indian paranoia about a Western military presence in the region grew. By 1987, Colombo was beginning to make headway against the guerrillas, at huge human costs. At that point India, now under Rajiv Gandhi's administration, made a move that shook the region. In June 1987, when the Jaffna peninsula was under pounding from Colombo's guns and its few aircraft, and the Sri Lankan Navy would not allow Indian ships to bring relief supplies to the besieged Tamils, the Indian Air Force violated Sri Lankan airspace to drop the goods over Jaffna. Later I was told in Kathmandu that it was then that Nepal decided to buy anti-aircraft guns from the Chinese. "The skies of South Asia are no longer safe," a Bangladeshi minister remarked later. "What the Indians did to Jayewardene they could do to any of us."

Within weeks, the Sri Lankan government and India were at work on an agreement that would allow Indian peacekeeping troops to be sent to the island to disarm the Tamil rebels while Colombo passed the necessary legislation to restore the Tamil language to national status and redraw the political map to give considerable autonomy to a Tamil region. It was not the Tamil Eelam—the Tamil nation—that the guerrillas were fighting for, but it was a huge concession for Sri Lanka, whose central government had never shared significant power with the provinces. The accord had a few originally unpublicized "annexures." India demanded, among other things, that Sri Lanka bar foreigners from the development of an oil-tank facility near the superb harbor of Trincomalee, where foreign military ships would no longer be allowed to call. New Delhi also ordered Sri Lanka to stop work on a proposed Voice of America transmitter. Sri Lanka's Sinhalese majority was outraged at India's bullying, and within months, the peaceful Sri Lankan south was in the throes of another armed and senselessly violent rebellion, this time led by radical Sinhalese youth, backed by a militant Buddhist clergy.

In a speech in 1989 to members of India's United Service Institution, a study center for high-ranking defense and civil service officers in New Delhi, J. N. Dixit, who was India's high commissioner (the Commonwealth equivalent of an ambassador) in Sri Lanka at the time of the Indo–Sri Lanka Accord, gave a clear and honest accounting of why New Delhi had intervened militarily in the small neighboring country. The speech was later published in the *USI Journal*. The first reason for the intervention, Dixit said, was to preserve Indian unity. "Let us not forget," he said, "that the first voice of secessionism in the Indian Republic was raised in Tamil Nadu in the mid-sixties." In other words, there was a concern that separatism could become contagious. Indian officials have always been adamant that they never intended to assist the Tamil guerrillas in partitioning Sri Lanka, and wanted to keep the movement within bounds. Members of the Tigers say they knew this was India's aim, but they thought that they could carry on the struggle to its final conclusion by themselves. That they almost succeeded, against not only Colombo but also the Indian Army, is a measure of their commitment and skill.

The second reason for Indian intervention, Dixit said, was strategic. The Sri Lankan Army and paramilitary forces were growing fast. They were being trained by foreigners, among them the Pakistanis, British "mercenaries," and "the two most effective and influential intelligence agencies of Israel, Mossad and Shin-bet." Sri Lanka's offer of facilities to the Voice of America, he went on, "would have enabled the United States to install highly sophisticated monitoring equipment on Sri Lankan soil, which would have affected our security in terms of their capacity to monitor our sensitive information for their own interests." The southern coast of India was vulnerable to infiltration, he argued. Finally, he said, Sri Lanka was buying arms "from countries with whom our relations have been difficult."

The third motivating factor was domestic Indian politics, Dixit acknowledged. "While morality and absolute norms should govern politics, in actuality it is not so," he said, before going on to explain that New Delhi had to pay attention to the sentiments of 50 million Tamil citizens of India who were demanding action to stop attacks on fellow Tamils in Sri Lanka. Tamil voters could not be ignored. And so an Indian peacekeeping force ultimately landed in Sri Lanka to insure that something less than independence but more than the *status quo ante* could be secured for the Jaffna Tamils. By the autumn of 1987, less than three months after the Indo–Sri Lanka accord was signed, the Indian Peacekeeping Force (IPKF in initialese) and the Tamil Tigers were shooting at each other. New Delhi found that having created Prabakaran, it could no longer control him. Flown back to the island from Delhi, where he had been meeting Rajiv Gandhi in July 1987, to endure a ceremonial but humiliating surrender of arms in Jaffna, Prabakaran spurned the offer of a political role in a new Tamil province, even with the sweetener of a cash grant, and soon returned to the jungle to resume his fight, while India looked for more cooperative puppets.

The Indian military adventure in Sri Lanka was a disaster in almost every possible way. Before Prime Minister V. P. Singh brought the IPKF home in early 1990, more than 1,500 Indians had died, the Tamil provincial government created by India had fled the island in panic, and the Tamils of the Sri Lankan north and east had turned their wrath away from Colombo toward New Delhi. Even the most loyal Indian soldiers were bewildered by the situation they confronted, Dixit acknowledged. "In moments of introspection, they were always wondering: This is not China. This is not Pakistan. Why are we in Sri Lanka?" Undisciplined troops took to firing indiscriminately when attacked. On patrol, they looted buildings and assaulted women. A hotel manager in Jaffna described to me how Indian soldiers had carried away all his imported cutlery and crockery and hundreds of pieces of hotel linen before returning with a truck to take a wooden desk. In the fishing village of Velvettiturai on August 2, 1989, Indian troops went on a rampage after being ambushed, killing 52 civilians and burning to the ground at least 120 houses. The IPKF, India had been telling the world, was in Sri Lanka to prevent the Sinhalese army from committing atrocities like these. The Indian government tried to cover up the incident by flying reporters to Jaffna and telling them a different version of the story, but the villagers' own account was circulating in the West, dramatically written by David Housego in *The Financial Times* of London.

Venkat Narayan, an Indian journalist who followed the Sri Lanka story for more than a decade, said: "I never felt more ashamed of myself as an Indian than when I visited Jaffna during the IPKF time. I could see the hatred in all their eyes." Narayan is convinced that the behavior of the Indian Army in the Jaffna Peninsula and the public humiliation of Prabakaran in the 1987 surrender of arms were enough to plant in the mind of the Tiger leader, an accomplished assassin since his teens, the germs of the plot to murder Rajiv Gandhi. The Indian police believe that Sri Lankan Tamils completed the grisly task four years later near Madras, in Tamil Nadu state, with the precision that made the Tigers famous.

The Sri Lankan episode raised troubling questions about the morale and discipline of the Indian Army just as Indian troops were being called on to take a more prominent role in combating separatism in Kashmir and in the Northeast, a region connected to the rest of India by only a narrow corridor of land. The Indian military presence in Punjab, already large, grew larger. In all three areas, reports of army attacks on civilians began to emerge. *The Economic and Political Weekly,* an intellectual journal, reported that units of the Assam Rifles had tortured, killed, or detained villagers at Oinam in Manipur state in 1987, and suppressed the story by keeping Indian human rights groups, journalists, and politicians away from the site. Large areas of the

Northeast are declared off limits for reasons of national security. But the reports of indiscipline were not limited to troubled regions. On July 4, 1989, troops from the Sikh Light Infantry and engineering corps were reported to have gone on a rampage at a train station in Rajasthan after a dispute over seats on a train to Ambala, a large military center. Passengers said that the troops destroyed part of the station, trampling and scattering the crowds that always congregate along platforms.

In an extraordinary and apparently coincidental letter to *The Indian Express* a few days later, an army officer's wife blasted what she saw as a demoralizing system in the officer corps in which "devotion to duty and the rigors of an army life have got converted into a life of luxury and living off the land on the pretext that everyone else in the country was doing it." The ordinary enlisted man, the *jawan,* was left with resentment to add to his deprivation, she said. "The poor jawan subscribed to the regimental fund from his meagre salary for senior officers to get pooped off on Chivas Regal, while he did not get enough money for his own condiments or extra messing to buy *papad* or pickle to make his bland army rations more palatable." Instead of getting tough military training, the troops "were employed as mess servants, gardeners and caddies for senior officers at army golf clubs" while their superiors entertained generals.

Manoj Joshi of *The Hindu* newspaper and *Frontline* magazine, India's premier defense correspondent, argues that the Indian Army is still the best trained force in the Third World. But in a comprehensive look at the Indian armed forces in *Frontline* in early 1991, he wrote: "There is little doubt that there has been a rise in the instances of moral turpitude among army officers for obvious reasons. An army can be as good or as bad as the society it comes from." Joshi pointed out, however, that the army was confident it had the resources to correct problems. Up to 55,000 Indians apply each year for only 330 places in the National Defense Academy, which Joshi described as "probably the best-equipped residential college in the country." It is one of three major institutions turning out Indian Army officers. In the ranks, there are also more than enough able-bodied volunteers for all the armed services. Officers interviewed by Joshi had only a few nagging doubts about the need to raise the level of technical education by giving more status to the training institutions and to people with special skills, among them computer scientists, who are often not adequately rewarded in a hierarchical system that continues to put too much emphasis on field command as a route to advancement. After the Persian Gulf war, some strategic analysts also began asking whether it might not be time to review equipment needs and battle strategies in the wake of the Iraqi defeat in the field. India, like Iraq, had been heavily influenced and supplied by the Soviet Union. Less than a year after the Gulf war ended, Indians were shopping for defense systems in Europe.

The morale and readiness of the Indian Army is crucial to New Delhi's ability to curb its most troublesome neighbor, Pakistan. This consideration was evident in the lengths to which New Delhi went to discredit the villagers of Kunan Poshpora when they charged the army with indiscipline in an area close to Pakistani territory. Since the deep psychological shock of Partition in 1947, when Islamic Pakistan (then including Bangladesh) went its own way, the two nations seem to have deliberately sustained an exhausting and counterproductive level of hostility that has come in the way of trade, scholarly exchanges and tourism, ordinary human contact between relatives and friends, and even the joint archaeological work that needs to be done on ancient historic sites in the Indus valley and its adjacent regions. Neither the contemporary Pakistanis nor the Indian people, sharing centuries of history and a similar culture in the broadest sense of the word, know much about each other and how they have developed in their decades of separation. Only along the border, where they watch each other's television broadcasts, is there a glimpse of life on the other side. Negative stereotypes have formed and nationalistic prejudices are fanned officially in both countries. If Pakistan is accused of fomenting separatism in Indian Punjab and Kashmir, India is charged with sending agents into Pakistani Punjab and Sind to stir up ethnic conflict. Indian officials craft and distribute evidence to prove Pakistan's evil designs on India, including maps (some of them ridiculous) purporting to show the sites where Pakistan trains and shelters Sikh and Kashmiri separatists. Once an Indian war-game scenario called Operation Topac was palmed off as a real plan of attack against India hatched in Islamabad under the late General Mohammed Zia-ul Haq, Pakistan's president, who died in a mysterious air crash in 1988. Though an Indian magazine exposed Op-Topac for what it was, many Indian journalists go on reporting it as fact. In this plot-ridden part of the world, many Pakistanis, of course, see an Indian (if not Soviet or American) hand in the violent death of General Zia-ul Haq, though there has never been any evidence produced to support this or any of the other sabotage theories.

There have been three brief Indo-Pakistani wars: in 1948, when Pakistani raiders tried to seize Kashmir; in 1965, when Pakistan again attacked India's northwestern border; and 1971, when India stepped into an internal Pakistani standoff to split East Pakistan from West Pakistan and create the new nation of Bangladesh. A formula for establishing a comprehensive peace process always seems to elude these two suspicious nations, although hopes were raised when Prime Ministers Rajiv Gandhi and Benazir Bhutto—the son and daughter of the last leaders to sign an Indo-Pakistan peace agreement, at the Indian hill station of Shimla in 1972—met in Islamabad in 1988 during a regional summit conference. But a series of conversations between the two young leaders produced nothing beyond glamorous photo opportunities. When I asked Gandhi in 1991 how he thought he might get along with Bhutto's successor, Prime Minister Nawaz Sharif, he said he did not know the man. But then he added, skipping over Benazir Bhutto, that the Pakistani leader he could have done business with was General Zia. He said the two were all ready to sign an agreement on the disputed territory of Kashmir when Zia died. Although Bhutto later told an Indian magazine that Gandhi had made the same claim in talks with her, Indian and Pakistani officials close to the last Gandhi-Zia talks denied that there was any such accord on Kashmir, only on the Siachen Glacier, farther to the north. "We were always told that the young Gandhi didn't want to concentrate on details," a high-ranking Pakistani official said after the Indian leader's assassination. That was the only way he could explain Gandhi's assertion that he and Zia had struck a deal.

Richard N. Haass, a lecturer on public policy at Harvard's John F. Kennedy School of Government and President George Bush's Senior Director for Near East and South Asian Affairs at the National Security Council, suggests that unlike other longstanding disputes elsewhere in the world, the Indo-Pakistani conflict remains perennially "unripe" for solution, and no amount of brokering by intermediaries or framing of proposals by the parties themselves will succeed so long as the relationship between the two nations rests almost entirely on rivalry and distrust, and there is no will to compromise. A reporter working in both countries can sense that this is the case: both peace gestures and war threats often have an air of unreality, although the latter are taken very seriously around the world because of the nuclear capabilities of the two nations. India is particularly dismissive of new ideas floated by Pakistan. Islamabad, which has been the target of United States sanctions because of an unregulated nuclear program, regularly offers to sign the Nonproliferation Treaty if India will do so also. Pakistanis down to the grass roots see American prejudice in Congress's willingness to punish them and turn a blind eye to Delhi's nuclear policies. India, which exploded a nuclear device in 1974 and makes its own missiles, says that the treaty is inequitable because it leaves the larger powers with their arsenals intact, an attitude that is coming under criticism as obstructionist even in some quarters in Delhi. The gadfly Ravi Rikhye wrote sarcastically in *The Militarization of Mother India* that "a lot of simple-minded people (Gandhians and foreigners included) who cannot understand the subtle workings of the Great Hindu Mind can't understand how our bombs can be peaceful and other people's bombs (particularly the American, British, Chinese and French) not be peaceful." The world fails to grasp, he says, "that we kill for peace; they kill because they are warmongers."

India seems unable to rest secure in the knowledge of its vast military and economic superiority over Pakistan. Islamabad, while it gloats over stories of growing military indiscipline across the border, is perennially fearful of Indian designs and believes that it has to be ever vigilant and armed with the most sophisticated of equipment to compensate for its smaller size and greater vulnerability. That Pakistan chose to arm itself with American and Chinese planes and weapons, and often takes foreign policy positions at variance with India's, are sources of acute irritation in New Delhi. As Haass most concisely phrased it in *Conflicts Unending: The United States and Regional Disputes*: "Pakistan refuses to accept Indian primacy and India refuses to accept anything else."

The creation of Bangladesh in 1971, which truncated Pakistan, seems even more of a watershed in relations among South Asian states and between India and the outside world as time goes by. The fatal confrontation between Bengali East Pakistan, the more populous part of the Muslim nation created in 1947, and West Pakistan, with its culturally very different mix of Punjabi, Sindhi, Baluch, and Pathan people, was triggered by West Pakistan's refusal to accept the victory of East Pakistan's Awami League, a Bengali nationalist party, in the December 1970 national election. The Awami League's Sheikh Mujibur Rahman, thwarted in staking his claim to the leadership of all Pakistan by President Yahya Khan and his foreign minister, Zulfikar Ali Bhutto, called in March 1971 for the independence of the East. India under Prime Minister Indira Gandhi, seeing the opportunity to break up and substantially weaken Pakistan, allowed the Awami League to set up its rebel headquarters and ultimately a government in exile in India's West Bengal state. According to the definitive scholarly account of that fateful year, *War and Secession: Pakistan, India and the Creation of Bangladesh*, by Richard Sisson and Leo E. Rose, an Indian legal expert wrote a declaration of independence for the Sovereign People's Republic of Bangladesh to be read at Baidyanath Tala, just inside East Pakistani territory. Indians helped the Bangladeshis organize training camps for Sheikh Mujib's guerrilla army, later named the Mukti Bahini, or Liberation Force, and set up a Radio Free Bangla broadcast center near Calcutta. Sisson and Rose say that on April 30, the guerrilla camps were turned over to the Indian Army. As refugees and recruits poured over the border into India, New Delhi evicted United Nations observers and foreign volunteers working on relief projects. When the United Nations Secretary General, U Thant, wrote to Yahya Khan and Indira Gandhi suggesting that a neutral United Nations force be stationed on the border, the Pakistani president responded favorably, but Indira Gandhi replied in an angry thousand-word letter attacking the international community for trying to bolster the West Pakistani regime. This attitude in New Delhi toward international involvement in Indian affairs, including the refusal to countenance humanitarian help, has persisted to the present day. When Tamils fled to Tamil Nadu and called themselves refugees, the United Nations High Commissioner for Refugees was not permitted to assist in establishing or running camps on Indian soil. Help from other international aid groups was also refused.

In December 1971, after Bangladeshi guerrillas had pinned down the West Pakistan forces in their barracks, the Indian Army attacked. In a war lasting less than two weeks, it routed the Pakistanis. Up to three million Bangladeshi lives had been lost in under ten months. India, which had that year signed its treaty of friendship with the Soviet Union, emerged from the war with a new grievance against the United States, which it had accused since 1965 of a "tilt" toward Pakistan, a charge also made briefly against Moscow when it increased its aid to the Pakistanis at about the same time to counter growing Chinese influence. During the Indian campaign against Dhaka, the Nixon administration sent a five-ship task force—the carrier *Enterprise* and four escorts—into the Bay of Bengal between India and Bangladesh. Sisson and Rose say that the reported movement of a Soviet naval force in the Indian Ocean may have been the most likely reason for the United States to make at least a pro forma showing. New Delhi and Indira Gandhi, however, took the appearance of the *Enterprise* as a direct threat, and it has gone down in Indian folk memory as such. Gandhi was unimpressed that the United States had frozen arms supplies to the Pakistanis, or that Pakistanis were convinced that Washington had deserted them in their darkest hour.

The gratitude of Bangladeshis toward India proved to be short-lived, as Sheikh Mujib, who came to be regarded as an Indian agent of sorts, established a one-party state and indulged in extensive corruption and high-handedness. In every election or coup that has followed, Bangladeshis have looked for an Indian hand; many distrust the Awami League's close ties to India, a factor that hurt Sheikh Mujib's daughter, Hasina Wazed, in parliamentary elections in 1991. New Delhi has occasionally lived up to those fears. When the tribal people in the Chittagong Hills of southeastern Bangladesh, many of them Buddhists, Christians, or animists, began to rebel against the loss of their land and tribal rights to encroaching Muslim Bangladeshis, India obliged by training the Shanti Bahini, or Peace Force, in neighboring Indian states as well as at a center for guerrilla warfare near Dehra Dun in the Himalayan foothills, where some Tamils and other insurgents from around the region had also received instruction. Rebels interviewed in India corroborated stories told by captured Shanti Bahini fighters brought by the Bangladesh army to meet reporters visiting the Chittagong Hills during local elections in 1989. The rebels said that they were trained not only in weapons and explosives by the Indians, but also in propaganda and psychological warfare.

It was after 1971, the former foreign secretary A. P. Venkateswaran says, that Indian intelligence agencies, led by the Research and Analysis Wing, commonly known as RAW, began to play a major role in India's regional policies. "Mrs. Gandhi had a feeling of infallibility after that," he said in a conversation in 1989 at Delhi's Center for Policy Studies, where he settled to write after being dismissed by Rajiv Gandhi. "She began to use the intelligence agencies more, and the more you use an instrument, the more dependent you become on it. Beginning in about 1984, RAW played a role in our Sri Lankan adventure beyond what it should have been allowed to play. In the end we killed more civilians in Sri Lanka than the Sri Lankan Army ever did. Under Rajiv Gandhi, RAW began reporting directly to the PM. They have access now that they never had before."

"Bigness fortified by a strong sense of ancient glory may explain India's relentless power drive," wrote Mervyn de Silva on the "5th Column" guest page of *The Far Eastern Economic Review* in 1990, after Indian troops left Sri Lanka. De Silva, editor of the Colombo journal *Lanka Guardian* and a friend of India and its intellectual establishment for many years, was bitter. "A unique heritage, from the Buddha and Ashoka to Mahatma Gandhi, gives this drive an aura of righteous manifest destiny. It is on such foundations that the structure of modern Indian diplomacy has been built. Coercive diplomacy, invasion, and annexation—Bhutan, Nepal, Goa, Sikkim—have ensured Indian dominance. As the founder of the Nonaligned Movement, a quasi-ally of Moscow, and an important market for the capitalist world, New Delhi has been relatively immune to the censure that such cold-blooded Realpolitik would have otherwise invited."

11

The United States
and India

As INDIA APPROACHES A NEW CENTURY with its Soviet relationship in tatters, it is having to look anew at the United States, a source of investment, badly needed technological assistance, and trade. For much of the older generation, the generation still in power, a realignment that is more than superficial—more fundamental than the mere reciting of a new mantra for a new age—will be very difficult if not painful. In half a century, a dense vine of resentment has grown over official India's window to the West. Its roots have many sources of nourishment.

Through decades of nonalignment and a close relationship with Moscow, a disdain for capitalist America not only sustained leftist ideologues and socialist economic theoreticians, but also suited India's high-caste ascetics and cultural chauvinists, many of them British educated, just as it suited the English aristocracy and intellectual elite. This is one of several areas in which the Indian caste hierarchy and the British class system have a good deal in common. Crass, uncivilized America was clearly up to no good; Indians began to look for Washington's fingerprints on every misfortune, and to treat every American overture with suspicion. The all-purpose theory of the Foreign Hand was born.

That is why, when Rajiv Gandhi was assassinated in the small town of Sriperumbudur in Tamil Nadu in May 1991, it was only a matter of hours before the CIA was blamed—and why I, the only foreign journalist at the scene, and an American, experienced a few extra hours of panic after the event, when mobs began to form. An absurd rumor had begun to circulate that an American spy satellite had been "hovering" over Sriperumbudur, something a satellite cannot do. *The Patriot*, a left-wing newspaper, announced triumphantly a few days later that "the assassination confirms finally, if confirmation was necessary, that India now tops the hit list in the New World Order." But the instinctive response was not confined to the leftist fringe. In the *National Herald*, the newspaper of the Congress Party and the Nehru-Gandhi family, a columnist dredged up a wishlist of CIA plots against India, blaming Washington for Indira Gandhi's 1977 election defeat and the rise in the 1980s of Hindu militancy. "It is now common knowledge that the secessionists in Punjab and Kashmir have the blessings of the CIA and its Pakistani counterpart, the Inter-Services Intelligence, and that they are being trained, equipped and financed by the two secret service agencies," the article went on. "And to top it all, investigations have revealed that the bomb which killed Rajiv Gandhi has the U.S. military markings."

Two months later, a new home minister, S. B. Chavan, publicly accused the United States of involvement in the Rajiv Gandhi assassination. When the United States ambassador, William Clark, was reported to have chided Chavan at a diplomatic reception, the minister called his accusation a "slip of the tongue." Foreign diplomats in New Delhi have learned to suppress natural and spontaneous responses to Indian tirades because it is easy to provoke unintentionally an official reaction that is wildly out of proportion, even when criticism is meant only to get a few facts in order. Fear of ruffling this extreme sensitivity breeds considerable caution among diplomats and other foreigners, who are often singularly lenient in dealing with outrageous, uninformed, and sometimes deliberately dishonest statements from Indian officials and politicians. In the Ministry of External Affairs, media opinion is manipulated by private briefings for favored reporters willing to plant stories embarrassing to foreign governments, especially the United States. At the height of the Persian Gulf War, for example, a respected journalist was persuaded to write in a leading newspaper that Pakistani and American troops were shooting each other in Saudi Arabia, a piece of baseless Iraqi propaganda that had already been floated and decisively denied in Pakistan, Washington, and the Gulf itself. The Indian journalist and the official who "leaked" the item were obviously not aware that it was old and discredited news—or did not care.

The Persian Gulf War, which unleashed a general mania of anti-Americanism—sobering to those who thought India might have taken a more considered position in the light of Moscow's changed attitudes and the closing of ranks against Saddam Hussein at the United Nations—led to an acerbic verbal showdown between a senior Indian journalist and a high-ranking British diplomat that provoked demands in Parliament for action against the envoy. Intellectual India was enlivened briefly by the debate, which began with an article by Praful Bidwai, a senior editor of *The Times of India*, that ranged hysterically over Western military history, concluding that the West had deliberately tricked Saddam Hussein into war. "The West's duplicity acquires a truly sinister dimension today," he wrote. Peter Fowler, Britain's deputy high commissioner in India, replied to Bidwai in a private letter: "Surely you do no good to India, let alone credit to yourself, by spreading wild conspiracy theories, which paint as a Third World underdog an aggressive military dictator with vast resources and a proven contempt for human life." Bidwai replied with another diatribe, whose final thrust was: "In any case, it is for us, not you, to decide what is good for India or does it credit and what constitutes good or bad journalism." The two letters were published by the journal *Mainstream* after the matter got to the floor of Parliament.

Rajiv Desai, the columnist and public relations executive who trained as a journalist in the United States, saw trouble coming within a month of Saddam Hussein's invasion and annexation of Kuwait, four months before the outbreak of war. "Deep down in the psyche of foreign affairs thinking," Desai wrote in *The Economic Times*, "is a residual anti-Americanism that was buried in the rubble of the socialist bloc. It bubbles over now and then." The Persian Gulf confrontation provided the opportunity for an overdue eruption. Iraq had been India's lone friend in the Muslim world when others began to condemn New Delhi's increasingly brutal response to Kashmiri secessionism. Most Indians knew nothing about Saddam Hussein. The Indian press had been silent or very low-keyed in reporting on Iraqi atrocities against the Kurds and on Iraqi uses of chemical weapons to such lethal if not genocidal effect during the Iran-Iraq war. Indian technicians and engineers worked beside Soviet counterparts on Iraqi projects; a few Indian reporters were beginning to suspect that not all of these projects were peaceful. When war came, Saddam Hussein would be held up in India as a victim of Imperial America, a "secular" Muslim with whom New Delhi could do business and a beleaguered friend of India with good credentials in the (already irrelevant) Nonaligned Movement and the (fast-disintegrating) socialist fraternity.

"The assault on the people of Iraq should now be seen as an attack on the people of the Third World as a whole," said a February 1991 open letter signed by about one hundred and seventy Indian intellectuals, a virtual Who's Who of Indian thinkers. "We suffer in sympathy the pain caused to the citizens of the beleaguered country." They were protesting the decision by Prime Minister Chandra Shekhar to let Gulf-bound American transport planes refuel in India en route from the Pacific. Proclaiming that the war against Saddam Hussein had now become "a war against civilized people all over the planet," the letter asked "all Third World nations to come forward to denounce the U.S.-led assault on Iraq and generate movements of solidarity in favor of Iraq's right to survive as a nation." Among the signers was the political scientist Ashis Nandy, who had been advocating that India's role in the post–Cold War world should be to serve as a center of dissent against American dominance.

"Why are we anti-American?" a columnist asked in one of India's most influential magazines, *The Illustrated Weekly of India*, at the end of the 1991 war. Well, it's because of our differing "civilizational legacies." India, of course, is Gandhian, characterized by "nonviolence, anticolonialism, sacrifice, moralism and tolerance," all noble ideals. "Contrast this with America's legacy," urges the writer, Rajdeep Sardesai, before plunging into a slightly confused rendering of America's sordid history from a popularized leftist point of view. "It is one where economic self-aggrandizement, often masquerading as moralism, has held the key. This has been the case right from the time the Pilgrim Fathers landed in 1620 in New Hampshire." Skirting the Revolutionary War, which might be mistaken as anticolonial, the indictment dismisses the abolition of slavery as "a convenient excuse" for the Civil War, then rises in a crescendo to the great sustaining myth of contemporary anti-Americanism: "In 1971, the US sent its Seventh Fleet to aid Pakistan during the Bangladesh War and even contemplated a nuclear attack."

Although American development assistance was welcomed in the first years after independence and a passionate hostility to America was not fostered as public policy until the days of the insecure Indira Gandhi, inevitable misunderstanding was written into early relations between independent India and the United States, in part because of the dissonance in personal relations. As India was getting on its international feet in the 1950s, a major voice in India foreign policy was V. K. Krishna Menon, whom John Kenneth Galbraith, Ambassador to India from 1961 to 1963 described in his *Ambassador's Journal* as "an eloquent, frequent and unsparing critic of American policy." When Krishna Menon, a high-caste socialist who had lived in Britain for many years, was finally sacked as defense minister in 1962, after India had been caught unprepared by the Chinese attack, Galbraith said he "laid down the line" to the embassy staff on how to greet the fall of their least-favorite Indian leader. In his *Journal*, Galbraith recalls ordering that there would be "no expression of satisfaction, however difficult this is to enforce on the soul."

A distaste for the United States and the American way of life pervaded the Indian elite, many of whom had adopted the arrogant (and usually uninformed) superiority of the British Fabians and other London trendsetters in whose company they moved comfortably even as they led the opposition to British colonial rule. Nehru, the quintessential Kashmiri Brahmin, was very close to Lord Mountbatten, the last viceroy, and even closer to Edwina, his wife. The journalist M. J. Akbar, a biographer of Nehru as well as a confidante of Nehru's grandson Rajiv Gandhi, is convinced that Nehru and Lady Mountbatten had a physical relationship of some kind, for which he offers some evidence: a "clinch" interrupted by a boy sent to announce dinner.

Whatever the reason for Nehru's subsequent trips to Britain, however, the prime minister continued to feel at home in London after independence, while he often seemed to be enduring rather than enjoying his infrequent visits to the United States, as Galbraith noted.

Nehru's sister, Vijayalakshmi Pandit, who represented India at the United Nations and served as Indian ambassador in Washington, told me that her brother "wasn't too fond of the United States—I mean the politics of the United States." Nehru was by 1957 a founding leader of the Non-aligned Movement, whose causes got consistent Soviet backing in the United Nations. His sister, who knew the United States better than he did, took a more generous view, presaging the attitudes of a new Indian generation now in the making. "My three girls all had their higher education at Wellesley College," she said, "and I met so much kindness from the American people, real kindness. Long before I became India's ambassador, Gandhiji arranged for me to go on a lecture tour of the United States, and that's what opened my eyes. I met many, many people of all kinds. Few of us had that chance."

Vijayalakshmi Pandit said that she was able thereafter to separate America from the American policies that India felt were inimical during the Cold War years when she was in Washington. "America is a difficult country, you know," she said. "You have to go along with them all the time. They don't like to sit and talk about things like the British do, for instance. Our way of life, our way of doing things, our political point of view is the best—that's what they conveyed to me. So my time there was quite difficult. But I enjoyed every minute."

On the American side, much damage was done to Indian-American relations by John Foster Dulles, Dwight D. Eisenhower's secretary of state and one of the most intransigent cold warriors. Dulles was deeply anti-Communist at a time when India seemed to be drifting diplomatically into Moscow's orbit. He was dismissive of Nehru's cherished project, the Non-aligned Movement. Although also a Brahmin of sorts, Dulles was in almost every way the philosophical antithesis of Krishna Menon, his contemporary. Two more difficult personalities could not have been put in the way of what could have been a natural relationship between two big democracies, albeit ones with differing world views.

Ainslie Embree, the scholar and diplomat, says that the personality factor is critical to an understanding of what went wrong in Indo-American relations, and that clashes of character were not confined to only a few leaders. "It wasn't just John Foster Dulles and Krishna Menon," he said. "Nehru couldn't stand Americans. He had the attitude toward Americans of the English upper classes, with whom he identified. They regarded Americans as sort of barbarians. But John Kennedy couldn't stand Nehru either, and Dean Acheson thought Nehru was the most difficult man he had ever dealt with."

Krishna Menon, whose vituperative attacks Embree believes reflected the anti-American prejudices of Nehru better than many Indians would be willing to admit, had perhaps the worst long-term negative effect on Indo-American relations because of the indelible impression he made on the wider nongovernmental American foreign policy establishment in the 1950s, "the Council on Foreign Relations types," Embree calls them. "Krishna Menon became for many during those years the symbol of India. Something very few people in India recognize is that the image of Mahatma Gandhi has disappeared from the consciousness of everybody here, except for the Gandhians, and what remains is the image of Krishna Menon and Nehru together, with their criticisms of American policies." It is a view of an obstructionist and hypercritical India that has pervaded not only foreign policy institutions in the United States but also the United Nations, where Third World diplomats say that they are weary of being lectured to by New Delhi.

Embree, who taught at Indore Christian College, a Canadian-supported institution in Madhya Pradesh, through the first decade of Indian independence, remembers how different the atmosphere was then. "When I first went to India in 1948 there was still a very considerable pro-American feeling that had come out of the Indian nationalist movement," he recalled, adding that it was a time of unlimited access to the Indian leadership, almost to the point that the United States appeared to be picking up the mantle of mentor from the departing British. "Americans were very sympathetic to the nationalists. Gandhi had been a great hero in the United States, especially in the churches. There were a number of prominent American missionaries in India who were supporters of Indian independence; some had been deported by the British colonial administration. There was no particular hostility to Americans as Americans in those early years."

The slide in relations began when Washington took neutral, or sometimes critical, positions on South Asian regional issues such as the dispute with Pakistan over Kashmir. India expected United States backing in its claims against Pakistan, which still holds large areas of what had once been an independent Kashmiri kingdom. "We tried to be even-handed, which the Indians took to be anti-Indian," Embree said. When India seized the coastal territory of Goa by force from Portugal in 1961, American objections were regarded as offensive in Delhi. Criticisms of the annexation of Sikkim in the 1970s were received in the same spirit.

"And there was our attitude toward China—everyone's forgotten that now," Embree said. "The Indians were very, very pro-Chinese after the 1949 revolution. They didn't really know anything about China; they had no connections with China. But this was the time of the great phrase "Hindi-Chini bhai bhai"—Indians and Chinese are brothers. Americans were opposed to the Chinese revolution. A lot of anti-American feeling in India came from this source, especially from the Marxists. Some people in very high places actually believed that that whole U.S. China policy was designed to be anti-Indian." When roles were reversed, and India became anti-Chinese after the 1962 border war, the United States was castigated for its eventual opening to China under President Richard Nixon, and for making what Indians saw as common cause with Pakistan and China against New Delhi's strategic interests.

Indian foreign policy experts add that the formation of two American-led alliances in Asia—SEATO, the South East Asia Treaty Organization, to the east, and CENTO, the Central Treaty Organization, on the Western flank—dealt a blow to Nehru's hopes of creating and leading a vast nonaligned Asian and African world.

"American foreign policy in this part of the world has been quite strange," said K. Natwar Singh, the former foreign secretary and author. "Except for 1962, when we got some help in the war with China, the dice have always been loaded against India. Since World War II, the Americans were always found wanting. They seemed to be measuring Nehru against military dictators in Pakistan, who had links with the Pentagon. India is a functioning democracy, but the U.S. always seems to opt for military rulers." This general view, however debatable, would be seconded by most Indians with opinions on foreign affairs. So would Natwar Singh's pithy description of India's international self-image: "We are too big to be camp followers, and too proud to be clients."

Such an attitude had a deleterious effect on American aid efforts in India, Embree said, reversing most of the pervasive involvement Americans enjoyed in Indian development in the earliest years after independence. "Another kind of anti-American feeling began in the sixties with foreign aid," Embree said. "Indians resented American aid. They always looked on it in terms of something that was being forced on them. We heard endlessly that our aid came with strings attached, whereas Russian aid had no strings."

In the post–Cold War world, it is unlikely that pleasing India will be high on the agenda of Western policymakers. The onus is increasingly on India, which needs investment and technical assistance that cannot be provided by Moscow, to make its case dispassionately in the West. Successive Indian diplomats in Washington are trying to build bridges. Karan Singh, Kashmir's maharaja before the abolition of royalty in India, was a controversial and short-term ambassador to the United States. A political appointee in the waning days of Rajiv Gandhi's administration, he was in Washington for less than a year, from August 1989 to February 1990. During that time he was criticized by Indian-Americans for his ambiguous role in the St. Kitts forgeries, and by some embassy employees for disregarding established procedures at the mission. Something of a mystic and self-styled Hindu philosopher, Karan Singh nevertheless took a hard look at how the Indian Embassy worked, and came back to India convinced that New Delhi was just not selling itself or its point of view effectively to Americans. When we met to talk about his brief experience there, he had formulated a kind of diplomatic guide to the complexity of America. It went like this:

"I didn't look upon my assignment as simply being ambassador to Washington, that is, to official America. I really looked upon the whole of America as my constituency. I identified six areas in which the embassy had to function. Six Americas. The first was the Administration, which means not only the State Department but also most of the Cabinet—the whole gamut. Number two is Congress, which is totally independent. It is extraordinary what sort of power the Congress has in the United States to initiate policy, not simply to pass bills. That's a very important area and I was at the Hill quite often. The third is the media. America is a nation that is dominated by the media. The two predominant media are of course television and the newspapers, but special newspapers, newspapers like *The New York Times* and *The Washington Post*. These two, at least for us in Washington, were critical. But wherever I went, I would call on the local newspaper. The fourth is academic America, including the think tanks. This is something that I consider in the long range to be of tremendous importance. If universities begin to lose interest in India, then ultimately, inevitably, the American public will also lose interest. I was astonished to find that area studies on India had shrunk in the last twenty years. Everywhere I went, I met the faculty, talked to the students and tried to revive interest. The fifth area is what may be called corporate America. Corporate America is tremendously significant because it involves investment. These are important people. That is the area where I think I was not able to make any major contributions because of the simple reason that important trade-related issues were pending. Sixth is the Indian-American community. There are 800,000 now, which means that they'll touch the critical million mark in the course of this century."

Karan Singh was upbeat about India-born Americans, and saw in them the best hope of better understanding between two countries, the world's two largest democracies, that may have more in common than they think. "Wherever I've been, and I traveled the length and breadth of the nation, Indian-Americans were integrated into the community. The first phase of immigration was settling down and getting jobs. Many of them are now top technical people. The next ten years, in the '80s, they concentrated on building their places of worship: temples, gurudwaras, mosques. Now in the '90s, their energies and their resources are going to be released." Karan Singh urged Indians to join in American politics and support centers of Indian studies.

Unfortunately, his people-to-people system works only one way. Few Americans are permitted to work or settle in India, even if their aims are altruistic and they have no intentions of taking jobs from Indian citizens. Those who come and crash in ashrams or overdose on southern beaches are held up as examples of what America has become. Not long ago, I was driving through a village near the sea south of Trivandrum, accompanied by an administrator from Kerala University. He drew my attention to an American hippie couple camped on the sand; a small white child with matted hair and a naked, insect-bitten body covered in filth played nearby. "I understand this is the result of all those broken families in the West," the administrator remarked, before moving on to a resort hotel to ogle Swedish tourists in the swimming pool. Features on ordinary life in the United States rarely appear in the press or on television. When they do, it might have been better if they hadn't. I once read in a newspaper that Americans "manicure, powder and shampoo" their house cats before "tying pink and scarlet ribbons around their fluffy necks." The Jews most of all, the article went on, "have a fad for cats and are crazy about kittens."

Indians living in the United States are often portrayed in India as the victims of racism and violence—not always a false story, but only part of a larger, more complex one about race and ethnicity in America. By contrast, Farhat Biviji, an Indian immigrant to the United States, spoke out against the Indian tendency to condemn American culture and believe there is nothing to learn from it in an opinion column she wrote not in the Indian press but in *India Abroad*. "The greatest gift that America has given us is the conviction that all humans are truly equal," she wrote. "America accepted us despite our different appearance and lifestyle. This country valued us not for our financial status but because of our talents and perseverance, and cherished us for our individual personalities." Then, echoing what some lucky Americans also feel about India, she added that life in the United States expanded the spirit and strengthened the character.

But as American power is unexpectedly, almost accidentally, enhanced by the decline of the Soviet Union, "the hoary old imperialist has been brought out of the historical archives" to be thrust anew into the consciousness of Indians, says the columnist S. Nihal Singh, who sees a resurgence of the attitude "that it is India against the world." As most nations on earth grow closer through better communications and old political conflicts are replaced by new international challenges and crises—the environment, the world economic inequities, and the health of nations in the age of a new scourge, AIDS, and resurgent diseases like malaria, polio, and cholera—India could have a significant role to play if it were willing. Individually, Indians are eager to join networks, share information, and make contacts everywhere. Officially, this is still not the case, and India can be counted on too often to block rather than facilitate collective international action. Indian delegates have disrupted the atmosphere of numerous environmental conferences with diatribes against foreign experts whose advice and crucial documentation are dismissed as neocolonialist ploys, new ways to dominate the developing world. Official India balks at signing international covenants and treaties on a range of subjects, will not (as demonstrated in Kashmir and Punjab) cooperate with human rights groups when the subject is India, and will not allow foreign or international humanitarian organizations to operate freely in the country even in times of crisis or disaster. The Indian political establishment has, in essence, still not chosen to align itself psychologically or spiritually with the immensely diverse international democratic community, which needs the Indian people.

As New Delhi makes new efforts to attract foreign investment from the industrialized world, the tortured sagas of several large international corporations trying to do business with India have been watched by doubting outsiders as weathervanes of Indian intentions toward its foreign partners. Investors have listened to Indian promises that life with New Delhi's incorrigible and corrupt bureaucracy will be easier, but they have also watched a corporation like Pepsico be put through unending hoops by government agencies egged on by Indian soft-drink and fast-food companies with money to spend on lobbyists. They have seen Du Pont wait, inexplicably, years for final clearance on a tire-manufacturing project that would generate Indian exports.

Perhaps the most complex and instructive of all the tortured cases of foreign corporations operating in India is that of the American company Union Carbide. For the better part of a decade, India consistently refused to conduct a full, impartial, and international on-site investigation into one of the world's most disastrous industrial accidents, the leak of deadly methyl isocyanate gas at the Union Carbide India Ltd. pesticide factory in Bhopal in December 1984, which killed more than two thousand people, with hundreds more dying since. Foreign companies looking at India say that the case has troubling lessons, first among them the precedent set by New Delhi in handling the Bhopal crisis: that the foreigner, having invested large amounts of money, had no fundamental rights to manage his property in India, while being subject to huge indemnities based on the corporation's earnings worldwide. Foreign industrialists call this a "deep-pocket" law. Moreover, the Union Carbide case showed that the international corporation could be denied all access to its Indian subsidiary in the apparent interests of covering up mistakes or sabotage by Indians, even if this nationalistic intransigence blocked urgent and necessary studies of a disaster in the name of accountability and future industrial safety.

More than fifty thousand pounds of methyl isocyanate were released into the air over Bhopal over two hours on the night of December 2, 1984. When Warren Anderson, the Union Carbide Corporation's chief executive officer, arrived from company headquarters in Danbury, Connecticut, within a few days, he was not only refused permission to see the plant, but was also promptly detained along with a technical team. For more than a year, Union Carbide lawyers and scientists were denied access to critical evidence at their Indian subsidiary's plant—all the people in charge of the Bhopal plant during the accident were Indian citizens—and could not examine tens of thousands of documents, including routine company logs, that might have shed light on and helped to reconstruct the events of that night of horror. The plant had been sealed by Indian officials. When documents were released from the custody of India's Central Bureau of Investigation, some had been altered to fudge evidence; the forgeries were clumsy enough to be obvious. Union Carbide charges that a cover-up operation began almost immediately after the disaster, but that the crude attempts to rewrite logs and falsify accounts would never have survived scrutiny if agencies of the Indian government had not in effect become a party to the deception. Seven years after the tragedy, a settlement of $470 million dollars paid to India by Union Carbide had not been disbursed; the money was tied up in political wrangles over the size of the award, though it had been upheld twice by the Supreme Court of India. When the Indian government offered its own smaller interim grants, hundreds of false claims were filed, many by people in no way affected by the disaster. But a statue of a stricken mother and child has been erected in memory of the victims, reminding the people of India what happens when they deal with a "killer multinational." There have been repeated calls for the extradition of Anderson, now in retirement.

Union Carbide officials, working with Indian lawyers and scientists as well as other international experts, believe they know what happened at Bhopal that night. They are convinced that a disgruntled employee, passed over for promotion to a supervisory job, poured about twenty-five hundred pounds of water into the MIC tank through a hose connected to a pressure gauge, setting off the fatal reaction. They have spoken to the suspect and others at the plant, who provide corroborating evidence. But Union Carbide's case, right or wrong, is unlikely to be heard in India, although the company still has hopes of reopening the investigation. A high-pitched campaign against foreign corporations, with "Killer Carbide!" as its slogan, has set the tone for the debate and left the impression that somehow this horrible accident was purely the fault of outsiders. Publicly, there is no other side to the story.

As India entered the critical last decade of the century beset by uncertainties, the magazine *India Today* surveyed the world around it and produced this editorial for the age. It said: "It is perhaps a singular Indian trait to look for scapegoats wherever the crying need is for brutal self-criticism. The last decade, in particular the Indira–Rajiv Gandhi period, was characterized by facile invocations of political demonology and mindless xenophobia in the face of problems that were in their essence, the creation of politics and politicians. For too long the country has been engaged in a search for enemies without having the political guts to confront the beast that lies coiled in its own belly."

12

Afterword

Victory to Mother India

IN HIS *DISCOVERY OF INDIA*, a revealing book written over six months
in prison in 1944, Jawaharlal Nehru sensed that Indians were hungrily searching for a sense of themselves and their nation as it moved inexorably toward
regaining the freedom that India—the Bharat of antiquity—had lost more than
eight centuries earlier.

> Sometimes as I reached a gathering, a great roar of welcome would greet
> me: Bharat Mata ki jai! Victory to Mother India! I would ask them unexpect-
> edly what they meant by that cry, who was this Mother India whose victory
> they wanted. My question would amuse them and surprise them, and then,
> not knowing exactly what to answer, they would look at each other and at me.

For nearly half a century (lately with markedly diminishing confidence)
Indians have been looking to their political leaders for answers. Nehru was
first to accept the challenge and set out to create a new nation in an image he
formed from his own sources of inspiration, a mix of Western rationalism,
Fabian socialism, and what many have called an aristocratic view of society,
unconsciously casteist but colored perhaps by a sense of noblesse oblige. It
was a lonely task. Within months of independence, Nehru's mentor and
alter-ego, the Mahatma Gandhi, was dead, victim of a radicalized Hindu,
Naturam Godse, whose shadow still haunts religious fundamentalism in
India. Gandhiji took to his funeral pyre a different vision of society: a village
India able to live on its own strengths and in a natural social harmony that

would obliterate casteism and sectarianism and solve human problems while they were still on a manageable local scale.

With the death in 1950 of Vallabhbhai Patel, a third towering figure of the freedom movement was also gone. Patel was the conservative: opposed to socialism, unenthusiastic about taking on a world role when there was much to do at home, and wary of India's Muslim minority, whose public pledges of loyalty he once sought. Three years after an independence drenched in the blood of Partition, Nehru was on his own.

If India's first prime minister and his colleagues had flawed vision, as Indians of various political and social philosophies now suggest from their differing perspectives, the most serious flaw may have been to emphasize the "hardware"—the steel mills and dams—at the expense of human "software"—the health and education of women and children. That is how Satyen Gangaram Pitroda once explained it to me. Sam Pitroda, as everyone knew him, was a naturalized American electronics expert who renounced his United States citizenship to return to India, where he became a technology adviser to the governments of Nehru's grandson Rajiv Gandhi and later P. V. Narasimha Rao. Pitroda's brief was wider than his title suggested: into his purview fell telecommunications, literacy, drinking water, dairy development, and oilseed production. It was Pitroda's belief that if a greater effort had been made to improve the lives of India's women, the population might be closer to 600 million rather than the 850 million it had reached in the early 1990s, and the scale of present problems would be that much smaller. Pitroda, who had been a businessman in Chicago for more than two decades, knew that there was no going back, however. Looking forward, he preached computerization with a missionary zeal, believing it was the only objective way to marshal resources and break the lockhold local power-brokers had over illiterate populations in, for example, the keeping of land records or voters' lists. This made him very unpopular with the many Indians whose hearts were with Bharat, the traditional nation, more than with an updated India, the name foreigners gave their land. But the Pitrodas of India cannot be faulted for trying to analyze when and where things went wrong, and what might be done to correct them.

Looking back over contemporary Indian history, many Indians and foreign scholars and friends would place the beginning of political and social decline outlined in this book sometime in the late 1960s or early 1970s, as Indira Gandhi, Nehru's daughter and heir, tightened her control over the dominant Congress Party and began to manipulate processes and events to consolidate what was becoming a dynasty. By 1975, when she declared the infamous Emergency to save her political power at the expense of democratic rights, it was clear to many ordinary voters that something ominous and chilling had taken place. Two years later, she was summarily evicted from office in an election; it was one of the high points in postwar Indian democracy's often shaky progression. There was a collective sigh of relief. But Gandhi came back again, taking advantage of divisions among her opponents. In many of her policies, described in earlier pages of this book—particularly in her dangerous tampering with local politics in Kashmir, Punjab, and more than half a dozen other Indian states—she seemed to demonstrate she had learned no lessons from her 1977 defeat, except not to let it happen again. When the definitive book is written one day on her use and abuse of power, honest historians will have to conclude that Indira Gandhi must bear much of the blame for what India has suffered since.

If her son Rajiv had any hope of reversing the trend toward the overcentralization and personalization of power, he never really stood a chance against the coterie of sycophants, hagiographers, fixers, con artists, and unscrupulous gurus bequeathed to him by his mother as the Congress Party's inner circle. Something of an open-minded internationalist by instinct, Rajiv Gandhi also inherited, as we have seen, a foreign policy establishment frozen in place and mentality in the heyday of Indo-Soviet friendship festivals and nonalignment at its least nonaligned. By the time Rajiv Gandhi died tragically in 1991, new questions were hanging over the Congress Party and the Nehru-Gandhi family about possible involvement in bribetaking and the banking of funds abroad. The inside story of the Indira Gandhi–Rajiv Gandhi years has only begun to be explored; it may never be written because too many Indian reputations are at stake. The people of India deserve better.

When he first took office after the assassination of his mother in 1984, Rajiv Gandhi shared much of Pitroda's modernizing vision and commitment to human resource development, in layman's language making life better for India's vast deprived majority. Ashok Khosla, the Harvard-educated physicist who gave up an international career to found the innovative Development Alternatives organization in Delhi, which produces simple technologies useful to village life, says that Gandhi seemed eager to listen to new ideas. Before long, however, Gandhi seemed to have lost the will to take on obstructive bureaucracies and old-school politicians. The young prime minister also surrounded himself with frivolous, high-living friends and inept or uncaring advisers who soon attracted the disdain and fury of the powerful Indian social policy establishment, part Gandhian—influenced by the antimaterialism of the Mahatma—and part leftist in its philosophical roots.

If history will some day come down hard on the legacy of Indira Gandhi, it may judge Rajiv Gandhi's early years in office, from 1985 to early 1987, as the time of most cruelly wasted promise for India. It was a time of refreshing new ideas in education, the economy, and the arts. But the hopes and the euphoria were short-lived. When Gandhi was defeated in the 1989 election, critics said he had squandered the largest parliamentary majority in modern Indian history because he was out of touch with India's silent majority, the people in villages and towns. The social scientist Rajni Kothari said at the time that Gandhi and his entourage had no comprehension of grassroots

India; his administration could have been a committee of international civil servants sent by those old bugbears, the World Bank or International Monetary Fund, for all its distance from the people. On the night he died, reaching out to grasp hands in a campaign crowd, Rajiv Gandhi said he never really understood why intellectuals dismissed his ideas as "elitist," especially his plan to create a nationwide system of boarding schools to provide a nurturing, cultural milieu for children from poor homes where there were no books or lights to read by and little food to eat. He had never learned to sell himself to India as more than the heir of Nehru and Indira Gandhi, more than the man who would hold the fractious Congress Party together only because the once-venerable organization's least innovative, most self-serving political hacks needed him in the chair. Gandhi also failed to deliver on his promise to reform and democratize his party and cleanse it of politicians he excoriated as powerbrokers before he had to call them back to "fix" enemies and fight off a growing political opposition.

It was left to Vishwanath Pratap Singh—once Rajiv Gandhi's liberalizing finance minister and later the political foe who brought down the house of Nehru for only the second time in forty years—to articulate the most radical social policies since independence. Armed with his mental charts and graphs, Singh would at the slightest provocation plunge into a discourse on the practical realities of Indian life as it had been structured by caste. The poor with a low caste ranking inevitably also have low social status and virtually no access to the levers of power, he would say, producing statistics and drawing three bottom-scraping graph lines in the air above his head: economic, social, and political. If low-caste people became richer, as some do in a changing economy, their status and powerlessness did not change significantly, because the walls of caste, unlike class, are ironclad. (That made it one rising line and two static on Singh's graph.) On the other hand, a highborn Indian could be very poor—the Brahmin temple priests encountered everywhere are one example—but enjoy both social privilege and access to power. (That's two rising lines and one static measure, an inversion of the chart that plots the economically rising middling and lower castes.) Singh's plan was to turn the system around through more affirmative action in federal job quotas that would empower the socially downtrodden at the same time it increased their incomes. The plan was doomed by that unexpectedly violent backlash that led privileged young people to street riots and self-immolation.

Another constituency was alienated. Another government fell. More Indians, on both sides of the affirmative action issue, were left feeling even more sharply that they were living in a political house not of their own design. This unease is not confined to Indian democracy. A similar sense of being left out of a system built by and for others has gnawed at the consciousness of nonwhite Americans or Britons and many other racial, ethnic, or religious minorities the world over. Balancing freedoms and rights, social mobility and social order, majority practices and minority demands, continues to be democracy's greatest challenge.

As India approaches a new century, many of its citizens, disheartened by politics, have joined an international trend toward the creation and bolstering of single-issue movements—on the environment, conservation, health, education, or consumer advocacy—and broader civic-action groups that seek to force government accountability or political change from the grassroots up. The growth of such movements is especially noteworthy and important in India because of the potential they have for overcoming some of the country's deep social divisions. Purushottam Reddy, a professor at Osmania University's postgraduate center in Hyderabad and a pioneering leader in environmental protection, argues that Indians have yet to develop a civic culture, a sense of citizenship that would lead them into collective social and political action outside the interests of caste or clan. In founding his shoestring organization, Citizens Against Pollution, he has tried to foster participatory attitudes cutting across old divisions. There are dispiriting setbacks. When environmentalists forced a local industry to pipe effluent away from a residential area, a significant victory for community action, miscreants stole the pipes, which were never replaced. But Citizens Against Pollution was not deterred.

There are other important successes. In Calcutta, Bonani and Pradeep Kakkar, one an environmentalist and the other an advertising executive, founded a citizens' group that in 1991 brought the first class-action lawsuit against the city government to the Calcutta courts. The group—People United for Better Living in Calcutta, known by its acronym, PUBLIC—sought to stop the inauguration of an extravagant fountain in a park called the Maidan, a construction that would consume six acres of open space and a large amount of precious electricity in a densely crowded city where neighborhoods endured daily blackouts. It was called, ironically, the Fountain of Joy. The park project opened anyway, because the city's electrical supply company brazenly ignored the judge's ruling on behalf of the citizens. Pradeep Singh Mehta, who created another action group, the Consumer Unity Trust Society, in Calcutta in the early 1980s, remarked that the whole episode only demonstrated "the insouciance and utter callousness of the city administration."

But the Kakkars (who will stop while out walking to chide people stripping low branches from city trees for firewood) discovered something heartening when they began their efforts to force better services from government: there were many people waiting in their dark Calcutta homes for someone to show the way. When the Kakkars and their colleagues, dressed in black, organized a candlelight procession through dimly illuminated city streets, Calcuttans came out spontaneously to join the march. In a city where political parties muster thousands of marchers and demonstrators by fiat or incentives, the commitment of the completely voluntary Calcutta March for Power was revolutionary.

"When power fails," an open letter from PUBLIC to Chief Minister Jyoti Basu said, "life comes to a standstill. Households become helpless. There is no water, children cannot study, people cannot read. Thrown into sudden darkness, hospitals turn into health hazards. Streets become dangerous. Two hours of power cuts a day amount to wiping out an entire month of our lives." There was no immediate reply from Basu, a Communist seeking re-election after fourteen years in office on the strength of rural development. Basu had largely neglected Calcutta, except for a few beautification projects paid for by private industry as a contribution to the city's 300th birthday. In Calcutta, telephones do not work, water mains are polluted, and the widely heralded building of a subway—India's first—soon bogged down in labor and property disputes, leaving Calcuttans with a twelve-minute service on the fragment of the system that got completed. But after surviving a stiff campaign fight and winning a new term as chief minister of West Bengal, Basu did turn his attention to city services. The voices of the citizens were finally being heard. By the next election, disgruntled Calcuttans in civic action groups, inhabitants of the country's most intellectually sophisticated of cities, could become a political force and therefore a threat to unresponsive leaders.

India, quirky and quixotic, proud and prickly, is very different from us in culture and tradition and yet very much like us in the political task its people set for themselves: to make democracy work as well as this system inherent in contradictions can be made to work in a diverse society. In the next century, numerically speaking, there will be far more democrats in the developing world than in the industrialized West and Japan. The closest kinship to the younger democratic nations should be felt not by the former colonial powers in Europe but by the United States and Canada, where populations grow increasingly more ethnically mixed and societies spiritually more complex. We need to make connections; many Indians would welcome them.

Strategically, politically, culturally, and as a great story of sheer human endeavor, India cannot be ignored as its nearly one billion people, their immense human potential still untapped, move toward the twenty-first century, still seeking good leaders to whom they can again cry, this time with conviction, *Bharat Mata ki jai!*

REFERENCES

Some useful books and periodicals, including those mentioned in the text:

Bhagat, Dhiren, and Salman Khurshid. *The Contemporary Conservative*. New Delhi: Viking, 1990.

Brecher, Michael. *Nehru: A Political Biography*. London: Oxford University Press, 1959.

Brown, Judith M. *Gandhi: Prisoner of Hope*. New Haven: Yale University Press, 1989.

Cambridge Encyclopedia of India, Pakistan, Bangladesh, Sri Lanka. Cambridge, 1989.

Chaudhuri, Nirad C. *The Autobiography of an Unknown Indian*. London: Macmillan & Co. Ltd., 1951.

————. *The Continent of Circe*. New York: Oxford University Press, 1966.

————. *Thy Hand, Great Anarch! India 1921–1952*. London: Chatto & Windus Ltd., 1987.

Embree, Ainslie T. *Sources of Indian Tradition*. Vol. 1: *From the Beginning to 1800*. New York: Columbia University Press, revised second edition, 1988.

Galbraith, John Kenneth. *Ambassador's Journal*. Boston: Houghton Mifflin, 1969.

Gandhi, Mohandas Karamchand. *The Essence of Hinduism*. New Delhi: The Navjivan Trust, 1987.

Gregorios, Paulos Mar. *Enlightenment: East and West*. Shimla: Indian Institute of Advanced Study, 1989.

Haass, Richard N. *Conflicts Unending: The United States and Regional Disputes*. New Haven: Yale University Press, 1990 (section on India and Pakistan), pp. 78–98.

Hasan, Zoya, S. N. Jha, and Rasheeduddin Khan, editors. *The State, Political Processes and Identity: Reflections on Modern India*. New Delhi: Sage Publications, 1989.

Hay, Stephen. *Sources of Indian Tradition*, Vol. 2: *Modern India and Pakistan*. 2nd ed., rev. New York: Columbia University Press, 1988.

Kakar, Sudhir. *The Inner World: A Psychoanalytic Study of Childhood and Society in India*. Oxford: Oxford University Press, 1978.

Kohli, Atul. *Democracy and Discontent: India's Growing Crisis of Governability*. Cambridge and New York: Cambridge University Press, 1990.

Kothari, Rajni. *State against Democracy: In Search of Human Governance*. Delhi: Ajanta Publications, 1988.

Lamb, Alastair. *Kashmir, A Disputed Legacy*. Hertingfordbury, England: Roxford Books, 1991.

Mazumdar, Amiya Kumar. *Understanding Vivekananda*. Calcutta: Sanskrit Pushtak Bhandar, 1972.

Myrdal, Gunnar. *Asian Drama: An Inquiry into the Poverty of Nations*. Abridged by Seth S. King. New York: Pantheon Books, 1971.

Radhakrishnan, Sarvepalli. *The Hindu View of Life*. London: George Allen and Unwin, 1927 (based on 1926 lectures at Oxford). Unwin Paperback. London, 1960, 1988.

Rajagopalachari, Chakravarti, translator. *Mahabharata*. Bombay: Bharatiya Vidya Bhavan, 29th edition, 1988.

Rikhye, Ravi. *The Militarization of Mother India*. Delhi: Chanakya Publications, 1990.

Singh, Khushwant. *A History of the Sikhs*, Vol. 1: 1469–1839. Princeton: Princeton University Press, 1963.

————. *A History of the Sikhs*, Vol. 2: 1839–1974. Princeton: Princeton University Press, 1966.

Sisson, Richard, and Leo E. Rose. *War and Secession: Pakistan, India and the Creation of Bangladesh.* Berkeley and Los Angeles: University of California Press, 1990.

Spear, Percival. *The Oxford History of Modern India, 1740–1975.* 2nd ed. Oxford: Clarendon Press, 1978.

Thapar, Raj. *All These Years: A Memoir.* New Delhi: Seminar Publications, 1991.

Thapar, Romila. *A History of India,* Vol. 1. London: Penguin Books, 1990.

Weiner, Myron. *The Child and the State in India.* Princeton: Princeton University Press, 1991.

Weiner, Myron, and Ashutosh Varshney, editors. *The Indian Paradox: Essays in Indian Politics.* New Delhi: Sage Publications, 1989.

Periodicals

Economic and Political Weekly, Bombay
Frontline, Madras
India Abroad, New York
India Today, New Delhi
Mainstream, New Delhi
New Quest, Bombay
Seminar, New Delhi, esp. no. 364, December 1989, an issue devoted to Mythifying History
Sunday, Calcutta
The Illustrated Weekly of India, Bombay

Miscellaneous Sources

S. K. Singh on Indian Heritage and Tourism, Sixth Som Nath Chib Memorial Lecture, Feb. 11, 1991. Text published by the International Fellowship Foundation of India, New Delhi.

J. N. Dixit on the IPKF in Sri Lanka, a speech reprinted in the Journal of the United Service Institution, July-September 1989. New Delhi.

Census of India, 1991.

A Study of Knowledge, Attitude and Practice of ISM Practitioners in the Context of Delivery of Family Welfare Services. Made for the Ministry of Health and Family Welfare by the Centre for Research, Planning and Action, New Delhi, 1988.

A Study of Science and Technology Manpower in India. Made for the Ministry of Science and Technology by the Centre for Research, Planning and Action, New Delhi 1989.

Human Development Report, 1990, 1991, 1992. The United Nations Development Program, New York.

Various reports on human rights in India by the United States Department of State, Amnesty International, Asia Watch, the Punjab Human Rights Organization, the Jammu and Kashmir People's Basic Rights (Protection) Committee, the People's Union for Civil Liberties, the People's Union for Democratic Rights and Citizens for Democracy.

INDEX

Barbara Crossette, a senior editor of
The New York Times, has been the
paper's deputy foreign editor, a
diplomatic reporter in Washington, and,
from 1984 to 1991, a correspondent in
Asia, based first in Bangkok and then
New Delhi. Ms. Crossette, who is also a
research associate at Columbia
University's Southern Asian Institute,
was Fulbright Professor of Journalism at
Punjab University in Chandigarh, India,
in 1980–81.

She won the 1991 George Polk Award
for foreign reporting for her coverage of
the assassination of Rajiv Gandhi.◆